SMALL BRAND AMERICA III
Special Hawai'i Edition

BY
STEVE AKLEY

Written and Published by:
Steve Akley

To my friends in Hawai'i: Mahalo nui loa!

Preface

I may have the greatest hobby in the world. I am a part-time writer who gets to interview owners of small brand companies which produce excellent products competing against large conglomerates on a playing field designed for the bigger companies to succeed. These small brand owners represent everything, which is great about capitalism and America in general. They have a dream although the odds are stacked against them. Through hard work, perseverance and a commitment and dedication to a quality brand, they can succeed. I can't help but think this is exactly what our founding fathers envisioned for this country!

Small Brand America III, Special Hawai'i Edition, takes us to our 50th state. Isolated from Mainland U.S.A., these companies have the added obstacles of sourcing ingredients locally and attempting to garner consumer attention from over 2,500 miles away from the bulk of the United States' population. More than just specialties for the tourist trade, these are real companies with products, which you very well may find superior to the megabrands you are so used to buying in your local grocery store.

Like its predecessors, *Small Brand America III*, takes us behind the scenes of these brands to meet its owners and to learn about the company's story and unique history. If this hobbyist writer does his job right, you should have a great appreciation and interest in each of the companies and its products.

After all, each one represents *Small Brand America*!

Table of Contents

Chapter 1: Beer...8

    Maui Brewing Co.

Chapter 2: Chocolate...18

    Original Hawaiian Chocolate®

Chapter 3: Coconut Peanut Butter.................................28

    North Shore Goodies

Chapter 4: Chili Water 38

    Da Secret Sauce

Chapter 5: Distilled Spirits 48

    Haliimaile Distilling Company

Chapter 6: Distilled Spirits 58

    Island Distillers

Chapter 7: Dog Treats..68

    Maui Dog Treats

Chapter 8: Goat's Milk Dairy Products 78

    Surfing Goat Dairy

Chapter 9: Gourmet Cooking Salts 88

    Sea Salts of Hawaii

Chapter 10: Fresh Juice 98

    Akamai Juice Company

Chapter 11: Fresh Juice 108

    Govinda's Fresh Juices

Chapter 12: Granola 118

    Anahola Granola

Chapter 13: Honey..128

    Moloka'i Meli, LLC

Chapter 14: Hot Sauce...138

Adoboloco

Chapter 15: Ice Cream 148

Tropical Dreams Ice Cream

Chapter 16: Ice Pops 158

Shaka Pops

Chapter 17: Kona Coffee 168

Hula Daddy Kona Coffee

Chapter 18: Mushrooms 178

Hamakua Mushrooms

Chapter 19: Passion Fruit 188

Aunty Liliko'i Products, LLC

Chapter 20: Rum 198

Kōloa Rum Company

Chapter 21: Salad Dressing 208

Hawaii's Special, Inc

Chapter 22: Salad Dressing 218

Minato Hawaii

Chapter 23: Soap 228

Kona Natural Soap

Chapter 24: Spices 238

Aloha Spice Company

Chapter 25: Wine 248

Maui's Winery

Author's Notes/Resources 258

Bibliography/Sources 264

Special Thanks 266

About the Author 269

Find Steve on Social Media 270

Love A Cat Charity – Honolulu, Hawai'i 271

Also by Steve Akley..272

Chapter 1: Beer
Maui Brewing Co.

MAUI BREWING CO.

HANDCRAFTED ALES & LAGERS
BREWED WITH ALOHA

Brewery – 910 Honoapiilani Highway 55, Lahaina, HI 96761
(808) 661 – 6205

Brewpub – 4405 Honoapiilani Highway 217, Lahaina, HI 96761
(808) 669 - 3474

mauibrewingco.com
brewery@mauibrewing.com

Established
2005

Leadership
Garrett W. Marrero, Founder

Products
Beer in permanent, seasonal and limited editions as well as a
full service brewpub

Sometimes, it just pays to do the right thing…

Garrett Marrero was born and raised in San Diego. In 2001, he and his family took a vacation to Maui, Hawai'i where Garrett immediately determined it was the place where he would one day be retiring. Technically, he hadn't even started his career, but the retirement plan was already locked-in.

In 2004, his job as an investment consultant took him to San Francisco. He was getting further from Maui and not closer, but the idea of life in Hawai'i continued to weigh on his mind. He still vacationed there, but it wasn't enough to satisfy his desire to make Maui his permanent home.

One of the "slices of Hawai'i" he would enjoy at home in San Francisco was a Hawaiian beer. The product was named after Hawai'i and has a presence there, but when he looked a little closer, he was shocked to find it was actually brewed on the Mainland. They were selling the spirit of Hawai'i without actually investing in the local economy.

He felt betrayed.

Then, an idea hit him. He had been a hobbyist home brewer. What if he joined the wave of microbrewers by starting a brewery in Maui? As he further researched the idea, he was amazed to find there wasn't a company producing true Hawaiian-made beer that was available for sale off-premise. Yes, there were a few microbrewers who sold their product onsite, but there actually wasn't anyone offering packaged product, which could be sold at liquor and grocery stores.

Drawing upon his experience as an investment consultant, he began to put together a business plan. His goal was to create a world class beer that was truly an authentic Hawaiian product.

Staying true to these ideals meant much of his plan was contrary to what someone with his financial background would propose. Rather than trying to extrapolate every cent of profit out of the business, his focus was going to be staying true to Hawai'i, the local economy, and its people. The only way he was going to try this endeavor would be if he could source as many local ingredients as possible and produce everything in Hawai'i.

With a distinct focus for his company and a business plan in place, he began to scout possible locations. Proving the theory "timing is everything," he couldn't believe a brewpub on Maui was for sale. It had just emerged from bankruptcy and suffered from a combination of general mismanagement (for instance, more taps were dedicated to national brands than the product they were producing onsite) and the fact five owners, each with their own take on the business, were involved.

Garrett was able to buy them out, and he went to work. While he and his stepfather had done some home-brewing, scaling up for commercial sales was far different than what Garrett had done at home. Luckily, the brewmaster stayed on with them after the five owners were bought out. He taught Garrett how to brew, and it was really a renaissance for him as well since the Maui Brewing Co. was focused on producing the best products possible.

There were plenty of challenges facing Garrett in getting started. Some of the local laws made it illegal to do business as Garrett envisioned. He found the local lawmakers open to working with him to assist in amending the laws so a true brewery could operate, not just a brewpub serving product produced onsite.

Just as he surmised in his financial planning, working in Hawai'i was difficult. Labor costs, ingredients costs and utility costs are the highest in the nation. For instance, CO_2 costs for a typical brewer on the Mainland run around 7 cents a pound. Garrett's initial cost ran around 97-99 cents per pound. He has since brought it down to around 43 cents based upon his volume, but it still remains much higher than competitors on the Mainland.

Garrett managed to overcome the hurdles and challenges of higher costs by sticking to his belief if you produce the best quality product possible, people will pay you a fair price for it. He didn't go into his business assuming he would compete on price with the global megabrands.

Maui Brewing Co. began entering its beers in contests across the U.S., and they gained the attention of the industry. Garrett had managed to work with lawmakers to change the law allowing him to sell packaged beer. With a plan to begin offering canned beer, he announced his intentions at one of the national beer shows. Reflecting back, it was a spur of the moment thing as he actually spoke before the plant was in place or a distribution plan was ready to go.

Having heard Maui Brewing Co. was going to begin shipping its beer, orders started pouring in. They didn't even have a case packaged, and it was already selling!

The story of their locally-sourced ingredients, the approach of traditional and non-traditional beer making (they have a blonde lager and an IPA on the traditional side, but also have a CoCoNuT PorTeR and wheat beer infused with pineapple in their flagship collection) and multiple awards seemed to intrigue buyers.

Today, Maui Brewing Co.'s beer is available throughout the Hawaiian Islands, 11 states and 4 countries. There are aggressive plans in place to continue to grow the brand with further expansion, but they currently on hold as the company builds a brand new brewery with four times the capacity of the current location. Maui Brewing is now shipping less than fifty percent of all orders received, so this move is definitely needed.

In addition, the new facility will offer tastings, tours, product and merchandise for sale 7-days-a-week (the current location only is open to the public on weekends). Visiting the brewery is a sensory experience where you can see the hands-on approach they take in making the product. In addition to seeing production and tasting the beer, a popular sight is witnessing the toasting of coconut for their CoCoNut PorTeR. No extracts are ever used by Maui Brewing so all of their coconut has to be toasted onsite. They toast about 12,000 pounds a quarter so this ends up being a large part of the production process.

Maui Brewing Co. also continues to operate the brewpub where individuals can enjoy a meal while sampling all of Maui's products on tap. Like the brewery, they can also see how product is made, buy merchandise and packaged beer as well.

Garrett's mom and stepfather help out back in San Diego. At live events they often represent the company interacting with consumers and offering samples of the product. Garrett likes to note that despite Maui Brewing Co.'s challenges in filling orders, he makes sure his hometown of San Diego always gets its shipments. Yes, it's an important market for company growth, but there's also the factor of giving your hometown a "most favored nation" status, which he really likes.

Long term, Garrett foresees the company evolving into a craft beverage company and not just beer. They currently are experimenting with a root beer and may be adding other soda flavors to the mix as well. Down the road, Garrett could easily see the company getting into craft distilling to further expand the product line.

Despite all of the success, Garrett notes the most rewarding part of running Maui Brewing Co. is creating jobs. He states that there isn't anything he likes more than telling someone they are hired. Currently, he has 65 employees and is continuing to add more as the company grows.

In addition to a great product, he has made Maui Brewing Co. a great place to work. He matches 401K contributions dollar-for-dollar up to 4%, he offers profit sharing for employees and health insurance. In-turn, his employees pay him back through a workmanship which shows they too are invested in the company.

The dedication to offering a quality product, made on Hawaiian soil with Hawaiian ingredients by employees who are treated fairly seems to be paying off for Garrett Marrero. Then again, when you do things the *right way*, it's amazing how often those things fall into place for you!

Maui Brewing Co. Photo Album

Garrett Marrero

Brewing

The canning line

Product ready to ship

The future of Maui Brewing Co. could expand into other product lines like the Island Root Beer they are now starting to sell

An artist's drawing of the new facility

The brewpub offers dining and a full selection of Maui's beers

Maui Brewing Co. product lineup

Chapter 2: Chocolate
Original Hawaiian Chocolate®

ORIGINAL

HAWAIIAN CHOCOLATE®

78-6772 Makenawai Street
Kailua-Kona, HI 96740
(888) 447 - 2626

ohcf.us
info@ohcf.us

Established
1999

Leadership
Bob and Pam Cooper, Founders

Products
Dark, Milk and Criollo Chocolate

Hawai'i *AND* chocolate, now that's a combination…

Pam and Bob Cooper like to say "chocolate is aloha!™." In fact, it's a catchy phrase they coined and trademarked. It encapsulates the spirit of their company which is based in their own private slice of paradise: a working farm in Kailua-Kona, Hawai'i.

Before they even started their business, some might say Pam and Bob Cooper had found paradise in North Carolina.

After all, it is a state known for a relatively mild climate. There are mountains and beaches all within a short drive. Bob and Pam lived in Raleigh, a growing city with plenty of opportunities for employment. They had a beach house and a house in the mountains. Still, as they looked ahead to retirement, they sought something else. It would end up being a whole new adventure in a paradise where the "retirees" would literally be at the cutting edge of a whole new U.S. agricultural industry.

So how did they get there?

Both Pam and Bob were born and raised in North Carolina. They met at a drive-in movie where each had been invited by friends. They dated for a little less than two years before marrying.

Bob managed a country club, and Pam was a bookkeeper for a jewelry company. They enjoyed vacationing in warmer climates during winters. After several vacation adventures, they ultimately landed on Hawai'i as their favorite and soon began exploring all of the islands.

They found Kaua'i to be a little too small for their taste. They felt O'ahu, with the congestion of tourists and business, to be too busy for vacationing. Maui's climate and topography reminded them a little more of California than a tropical getaway. For them, Hawai'i, a.k.a. The Big Island, was perfect. With its farming, hospitality, natural beauty and laid-back persona, it felt like home and vacation at the same time. Once they had completed their comparison, and enjoyed the magic of The Big Island, they made it their only vacation destination from that point forward.

In 1996, Pam and Bob were looking to make a change. They believed the time was right to retire from their jobs and pursue a full-time move to their favorite vacation destination. The market was friendly for buyers at the time. Still, real estate was considerably higher than their home State of North Carolina.

They found a farm which would require them to sell all three of their homes just to afford it, and still they weren't sure they would have enough for the purchase price. They would have to make an offer considerably lower than what the seller was asking. Wondering if they could make it if the seller would accept, they submitted their offer in November of 1996.

To their delight, the seller did accept, and they began consolidating their real estate holdings to make the purchase. In March of 1997 they made the move from Raleigh to their farm in Kailua-Kona, Hawai'i.

There was a caretaker on the farm, and he would attend to the macadamia nut, coffee and cacao that grew on the farm. There was a small income from these, but Pam and Bob would need to seek employment to sustain their new life in Hawai'i.

Their first opportunity came from a business they started, the Hawaii General Store. This online-only shop catered to tourists who wanted a taste of Hawai'i by offering locally produced goods. The Coopers were probably ahead of their time with this offering as they had it running in 1997 and 1998, long before internet shopping was the norm it is today.

When it became apparent the Hawaii General Store wasn't going to be their key to maintaining their life in Hawai'i, Bob and Pam looked back to the farm. Perhaps there was a way to utilize resources already at their disposal. After researching the chocolate industry, they were surprised to find no one was utilizing the locally grown cacao to produce chocolate in the United States. There literally was no U.S. grown and produced chocolate being made. They were just adventurous, or perhaps naïve, enough to see if they could make a go of it.

Producing chocolate from cacao is a labor intensive proposition. The fruit is in continual bloom so you must constantly harvest it all year long. The beans are then removed from the pod and placed in a "sweatbox" where the process of removing the natural moisture in the beans begins. They are sun dried, and then the beans can be stored in burlap bags until chocolate production begins.

The process to make the chocolate begins with roasting in a process very similar to the roasting of coffee beans. The beans are shelled, and the inside is crushed into a mix known as "nibs." The nibs are then crushed to make what is known as chocolate liquor. At this point, sugar is added for dark chocolate. If you are making milk chocolate, sugar, vanilla and milk are introduced. The mixture is then stirred slowly as the temperature is reduced to the point where it can be poured into molds to make the final product. In addition to the hands-on labor which goes into making chocolate, specialized machinery is required each step of the way.

Knowing they would have to utilize the buildings already on the farm (their land was leased so any new structures would have to be approved by both the county and the lessor… a proposition not likely to happen), Pam and Bob began to research the viability of starting their own chocolate business. Their first step was to hire a consultant to see if they really had an opportunity there.

They were lucky to secure a well-respected chocolatier from England. He came to Hawai'i to teach them what they would need to do each step of the way to take their harvest and produce chocolate. Additionally, he helped them by sending their beans out for testing in Barcelona, Spain.

With the knowledge gained from their consultant, and a test that came back "bold and forthright" for the flavor of their cocoa beans, the Coopers were ready to start the Original Hawaiian Chocolate Company.

The next step was to secure the equipment they needed. This wasn't as easy or as simple as just reaching out to a manufacturer with a list of machinery needs. The size limitations they had meant their business was going to be on a much smaller scale than the typical chocolate company. This wasn't because they were just starting their business, it also went back to their space limitations on the farm.

Their intensive search led them to tracking down all leads on the smallest chocolate equipment they could find. It also often meant they would have to find them globally and then retro-fit them so they would work in the United States.

Suddenly, Pam and Bob weren't two retirees simply living in paradise. They were owners who were involved in every aspect of their business. With no blueprint to help them out (again, there were no other U.S. companies doing what they were doing), they literally figured out their business via trial and error.

Fortunately, their successes far exceeded their setbacks. As they began to produce their chocolate, the response they were getting was incredibly positive. To say people *loved* the bold flavor and satiny texture of their home-grown-and-made chocolate would be an understatement. They also opened their farm to tours which offered consumers live demonstrations of chocolate production. Despite the passion individuals have for chocolate, for the most part they do not know how it's produced, so the Coopers' farm offered them a unique experience to see and taste exactly how chocolate is made.

To their credit, the Coopers really wanted to make this a new industry for the State of Hawai'i. Cacao only grows 15 – 20 degrees north or south of the equator meaning Hawai'i is the only place in the U.S. where it could be grown. They believed it was a unique opportunity to start a new agriculture product for the State; a way of giving back to the State they love so much.

Despite their efforts, they didn't get a lot of interest in developing chocolate products as a local industry, so they invested their efforts in making their own chocolate the best it could be.

As they got into more stores and local chefs began to incorporate their chocolate into signature desserts, people did begin to take notice. When celebrity chef Alton Brown brought his show *Good Eats*™ to the farm, people certainly recognized the value of U.S. produced chocolate.

Today, the future looks very bright for Pam and Bob Cooper and their Original Hawaiian Chocolate. There is a real buzz about their product, and their dream of starting a new industry for Hawai'i has been realized as other competitors are beginning to enter the market.

Bob and Pam don't worry about the competition; they welcome it. After all, chocolate is aloha, and there is plenty of aloha in Hawai'i!

Pam and Bob Cooper

Cacao pods

A pod opened to expose the cocoa beans

Cocoa beans drying in the sun

Roasting the cocoa beans

It's chocolate!

Bob leading a tour

Original Hawaiian Chocolate® product lineup

Chapter 3: Coconut Peanut Butter
North Shore Goodies

Flagship Store:
66-216 Farrington Highway, Unit #100, Waialua, HI 96791

Main Production Facility/Second Store:
94-1338 Moaniani Street, Unit #112, Waipahu, HI 96797

(808) 637 - 515

northshoregoodies.net
neverleavehawaii@aol.com

Established
2008

Leadership
Marc and Ruth Bryner, Owners

Products
Coconut peanut butter in multiple flavors and a variety of made in Hawai'i goodies, including: pancake mix, naturally flavored syrups, cake mixes, salad dressing, barbecue sauce, coffee and more

Going to work every day with a smile on their faces…

There is little doubt, hard winters and a frantic lifestyle can take their toll. They can literally take the smile right off of your face.

Just ask Ruth and Marc Bryner. After raising two kids in Chicago, and a career in the printing business for Marc, they were done. The stress of living in the big city had them fried.

With their children moved out of the house, they were free to do whatever they wanted. For most people, considering a move to Hawai'i would be a huge, life-changing event which would be carefully thought out and orchestrated.

Marc and Ruth took a different approach. They knew they loved Hawai'i from vacations, and they clearly wanted to move there. The approach for them wasn't a carefully thought out plan, though. They decided just to go for it.

They secured a place to live and simply moved. They knew they would need to work, but they didn't pursue securing employment while they were still in Chicago. They just assumed everything would fall in place when they got to Hawai'i.

After the mandatory "chill-time" of just hanging out when you get to Hawai'i, Marc decided he needed to start to do something to earn a living. He was done with the printing business… that much he knew.

He decided to go back to an earlier dream. One he hadn't actually followed through. He actually had his Masters in Culinary Arts but hadn't pursued a career in food because the opportunity with the printing company came up.

His idea to enter into the culinary field was to grill hot dogs and sell them on the beach in North Shore. Getting into the food business sparked a passion for him. He began experimenting with local ingredients and trying out recipes on friends. One became a big hit with friends and neighbors. His coconut peanut butter, which was simply fresh coconut and peanuts, was getting raves from anyone he'd let try it.

He thought he was onto something, so he began preparing it in a commercial kitchen and jarring it. He was then going to sell it at the local farmers' market.

He took his new product to the market and it sold out. Of course, he went back and prepared more and headed back to the market. He had repeat customers looking for him when he returned.

A group of flight attendants requested he make a chocolate coconut peanut butter, so he did. It too began to sell very well at the market. Now the floodgates were open. He was experimenting with different flavor combinations for his peanut butter, and he began trying other products as well.

His next offering was pancake mix, using locally sourced fruits to add flavor.

Guess what?

Yes, it was another winner. When you have a pancake mix line, you have to have syrups.

The central theme to every line Marc would launch was it had to have a Hawaiian tie-in to classic products. Then he would expand each line to offer multiple flavor choices for each. For example, his syrup line now has a Macadamia Nut, Guava, Vanilla Bean, Liliko'i (passion fruit) and Coconut.

As he added more products, he soon had a need to have his own commercial kitchen. They opened up a combination kitchen and storefront in Waialua, the North Shore area of O'ahu.

Ruth also joined in the business. She does all of the bookkeeping. Business has been so good both of their children have joined them in Hawai'i, and they are helping out now as well.

Although they now had their own store, they continued to work farmers' markets around town. One day an individual approached Marc. He was very interested in Marc's product lines and personal story. He didn't give any details, but he told Marc if he liked the items he bought he would reach out to him about an "opportunity" he had.

Honestly, Marc didn't think a whole lot about the situation. If something was meant to be, he figured it would happen. If not, he was as busy as he could be anyway. With no details shared as to what the "opportunity" was, he really didn't feel like he had anything to lose in the situation.

True to his word, the man from the farmers' market called him back. He was with a company involved in many of the award shows you see on TV. He wanted to get North Shore Goodies' products into the "schwag bags" given to celebrities at these events. He was ready to hook up Marc for both MTV's Video Music Awards™ and the Country Music Awards™.

Marc jumped at the chance and soon his clientele was shifted to a heavily celebrity-laden group. His relationship with his original contact has grown to the point where they are now involved in almost every awards show you can imagine. In 2014, that even means the granddaddy of all awards shows, the Oscars™.

Now, it's so common, the staff doesn't even blink an eye when a well-known celebrity calls the store to make a purchase or someone pops in. Their celebrity clients remain a closely guarded secret to maintain their privacy, but a quick Google® search shows celebrity after celebrity holding up packs of North Shore Goodies at these star-studded events.

Having the buzz of celebrity connections also helps distribution. The company has secured distribution in about 80 stores on the Mainland, all based on their requests to sell North Shore's products.

Business has been so strong, they outgrew their kitchen at their original store. They opened a second facility in Waipahu about 30 minutes away. This increased their retail space at the flagship store, and they even opened up a smaller store at the new production site.

Marc has maintained a focus just on his products at the stores. He has avoided the pitfalls of adding lines of "tourist trap" souvenirs which seem to be in every other store in Hawai'i. He has had to make one concession, though. Ruth collects shells and other items she finds at the beach and makes some craft/art products. There is no way Marc is able to tell his wife he isn't carrying her line of items, so the store remains just North Shore Goodies food items and "Art by Ruth."

Today their business mix is fairly diverse in terms of how it is broken-up. They do about 1/3 of their business via each of these segments:

- Retail through their stores and website
- Wholesale to other stores which sell their products
- Farmers' markets.

Ruth and Marc still do not look too far into the future. They aren't pining over charts and graphs to see how they are doing now versus projections, forecasts and pivot tables. They like taking each day as it comes and having fun.

They state their goal is simple: put smiles on the faces of their customers. They want to make great products their customers can enjoy. When they do their job right, they have happy customers who become part of their extended family.

As far as the Bryners themselves?

Well, let's see. They don't have to deal with the traffic, weather and congestion of Chicago. They wake up every day in paradise, and they have a business which is gaining a great deal of respect and solid base of loyal customers.

It's not surprising that Marc's and Ruth's faces are in a permanent state of smiles!

North Shore Goodies Photo Album

Marc Bryner

North Shore Goodies offers its peanut butter in multiple flavors

North Shore Goodies products on the shelf of their store

The only non-food items sold at North Shore Goodies are crafts made by Ruth (notice the "Look what I made sign on the end)

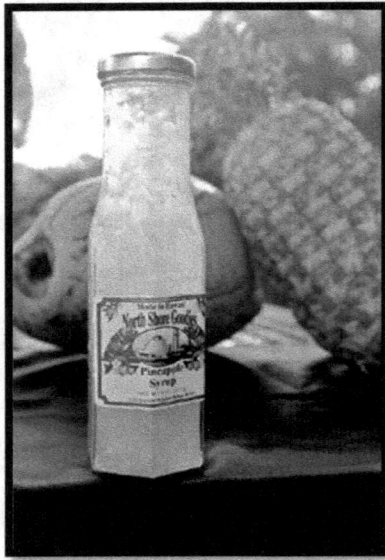

North Shore Goodies' product lineup includes product such as pineapple syrup…

…and Coconut Syrup

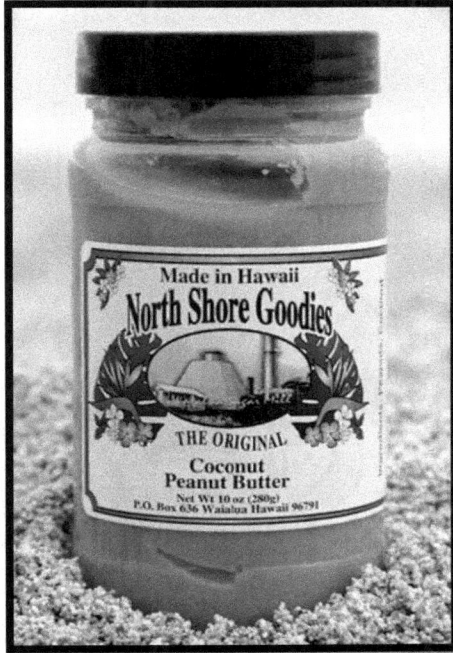

Coconut peanut butter remains North Shore Goodies signature product

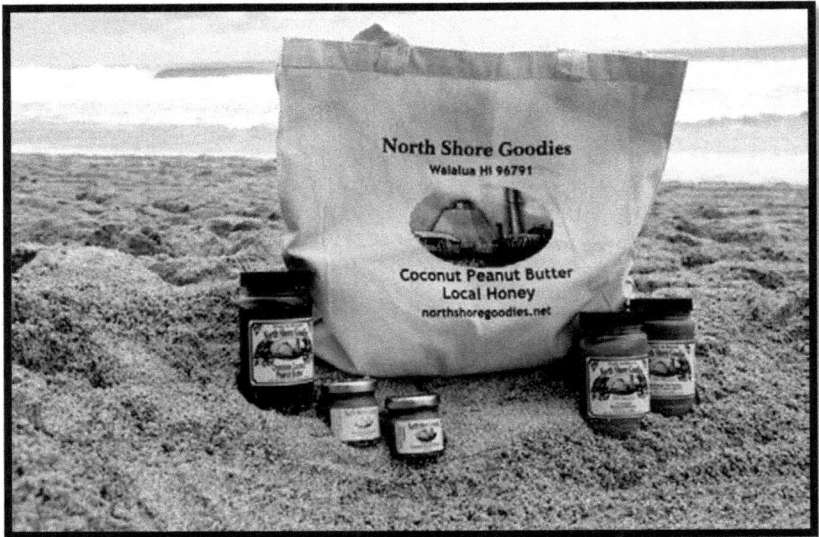

North Shore Goodies product lineup

Chapter 4: Chili Water
Da Secret Sauce

dasecretsauce.com
dasecretsauce@gmail.com

Established
2012

Leadership
Rex Moribe, Owner

Products
Da Secret Sauce Chili Water

Not a marketing scheme, or just a product, Rex Moribe is introducing you to his heritage...

Chili water is not hot sauce.

There are many similarities which may lead to confusion, but if you look close enough, you will see they are totally different products. On the similar side, they each are sauces to add to food. Peppers are the base ingredient for both hot sauce and chili water. They add a level of heat, but should complement the flavor profile not overpower it ("overpowering" is individual taste so there are different levels of heat for both hot sauce and chili water).

Chili water is light to clear in color and is as thin as water. Hot sauce is most commonly red in color and has a much thicker viscosity than chili water (ranging from the consistency of a thin to a thick spaghetti sauce, depending on the brand).

While Louisiana may be ground zero for hot sauce production in the United States, it is made elsewhere in the U.S. and around the globe. The production of, appreciation of, and knowledge of chili water is basically confined to one place in the world: Hawai'i.

There is no record as to when chili water became a cultural icon in Hawai'i; but if you ask people in the know, they will say it has an Asian influence from the workers coming to Hawai'i to work in the sugarcane fields. Soon the locals started mirroring these unique sauces the workers in the sugarcane fields would use to spice up their dishes.

When Rex Moribe was growing up on Kaua'i, everyone he knew had their own version of chili water at their house. This was simply part of what they did as a family. They would grow their own peppers and develop the flavor profile to their unique specifications. As soon as he was old enough to put ingredients together himself, Rex began taking the best of his relatives' recipes to make his own version of chili water.

Soon it seemed his version of chili water was the most popular in the family. It wasn't uncommon for relatives to ask if he would be bringing his "secret sauce" to family gatherings.

Selling chili water wasn't anything Rex had envisioned for himself. In fact, he thought his future was set. He was into bodyboarding; world-class, competitive bodyboarding. He had a sponsor and dreamed of doing it for a living for the rest of his life. He moved to O'ahu as soon as he turned 18 to position himself in the center of the bodyboarding community in Hawai'i.

The problem was as good as Rex was, among the top bodyboarders in the world, there simply wasn't the respect or opportunities as there were in surfing. He was chasing a dream, but the upside was limited, and his family wanted a more traditional, stable and certain future for him. In fact, his grandfather's dying wish was for Rex to give up bodyboarding and to go to college.

Rex made the promise he would do exactly that for his grandfather, and he was true to his word. He gave up bodyboarding and went to college. He graduated with two associate degrees, one in business and one in information technology. He landed a job as an IT administrator and started his conventional life.

When a co-worker mentioned she was involved in producing feature films (running a company on the side called Sandust Productions™), Rex was intrigued. He always had an interest in movies. He told her he would like to make a movie himself. She thought she would scare him off by telling him she would help him, but he would need to produce a script before they got started.

Within two weeks Rex surprised her with a script for a full-length movie. She agreed to help get it off the ground and provide some of the support he needed to make the movie if he would help with another film she was working on. After serving as a gopher on the set of that movie, Rex was ready to make his feature film debut.

Rex was successful in pulling off something few do. He wrote and directed a feature length film entitled, **One Night Many Moments**. Ultimately, he wasn't successful on the film festival circuit, and he didn't land a distribution deal, but it was a great experience for him.

While things were going smoothly with his job as an IT administrator, Rex was not the type to sit around or just do one thing. After moving to O'ahu, he had been surprised how individuals didn't have the love for chili water as they had in Kaua'i. He was amazed in many cases people hadn't even heard of it there.

Even going back home to Kaua'i over the years, he seemed to find less and less of his own family keeping a jar of chili water around. This made his own "secret sauce" blend even more popular at family gatherings.

He began to think there may be an opportunity to make chili water and sell it. In 2007, he launched Da Secret Sauce using his unique chili water recipe and a name spun from family member's requests for his "secret sauce." He was amazed at how people took to it. People began to talk about how much chili water had been part of their family life. Old timers loved to share stories with him about their own unique blends they used to have at their houses.

It was looking like it was a great venture as he was able to keep his job and produce and sell his chili water in his spare time. Tragedy struck in 2008 when his father passed away. Shocked and saddened to the core, Rex was stripped down to survival mode. He didn't have the time, effort or passion to put into a hobby business with the hurt he had for the loss of his father. He simply shut Da Secret Sauce down and continued working his IT job.

In the subsequent years after 2008, chili water had a bit of resurgence on the Hawaiian Islands. It seems the younger generation discovered chili water, and they looked to bring back the craft of making it. As it became popular again, more companies began producing it, and restaurants began offering it again to customers.

People kept asking Rex if he was going to bring back his Da Secret Sauce chili water. In 2012, he finally relented. This time, he was determined to not only make it, but also do everything systematically and by the book. The first time around, he had been making batches at his home and bottling them himself. This time he wanted to make a truly commercial product he could sell in stores.

He began working with the FDA and the Department of Health in Hawai'i. He soon got on a first name basis with his representatives from both as he worked through all of the issues he would need to get his product on the market.

When it came time to design his label, he found a website offering a contest for graphic designers. You tell them your company name and provide ideas on what you like, and they design a logo for you. Any of their designers then can submit a prototype for you to choose from over the course of seven days. At that time, you can narrow it down to 10, have them refine their designs to your specifications, and then you finally select a winner. Rex was amazed to have over 250 designs come in. He literally printed every one of them, bottle-sized, to see which one would jump from the shelf. While he liked many of the designs, he finally chose the one he believed was the clear-cut winner.

Once he had his logo design, packaging and formulation approved by the FDA and the Hawaiian Department of Health, he was in business. He found a co-packer to produce his product in a commercial kitchen. He then started getting it into stores, one at a time. He found the process to be surprisingly easy once he got into Hawaiian Fire®, his first store. He just referenced they were carrying his chili water, then the doors opened for the next store, where he then told the next store he was in those two stores, they let him in, etc.

Today, Rex's biggest challenge isn't getting distribution for his product or selling his inventory, it is securing enough peppers to make his product. His recipe, refined from his own family traditions, uses only a specific pepper called Hawaiian Peppers. He's currently using 100% of his inventory from his two growers: his mother and a farmer on The Big Island. Since he hasn't been able to find another source for these peppers, you might think he would look to refine his recipe using a more commonly available alternative. This isn't something Rex is willing to compromise on, though. He stresses the fact this is his heritage. This isn't a by-product of a marketing effort. He is selling the recipe of his family. The Moribe family only used Hawaiian Peppers, and it's the only pepper he will ever use in his product, even if it tempers his ability to grow his business.

Things are going so well, Rex has even brought back his love for movie making. He actively makes short videos of travel, extreme sports and fun scenarios which help him promote his chili water business. He's looking to give another shot at feature films. He's doing some pre-production on a documentary he's been thinking about for a long time.

The re-launch of Da Secret Sauce has been great. He has gotten tons of press, including two features in Hawaiian Airlines® in-flight magazine. He has accounts all across Hawai'i and even on the Mainland in San Diego and one in Japan. He's also helping his first passion by sponsoring a bodyboarder!

The shortage of Hawaiian Peppers seems to be the only stumbling block. He's looking to create industry in his home state and introduce people to his family traditions. He just needs the raw ingredients to do it.

If you are a farmer, and you want to grow Hawaiian Peppers, call Rex Moribe… immediately!

Da Secret Sauce Photo Album

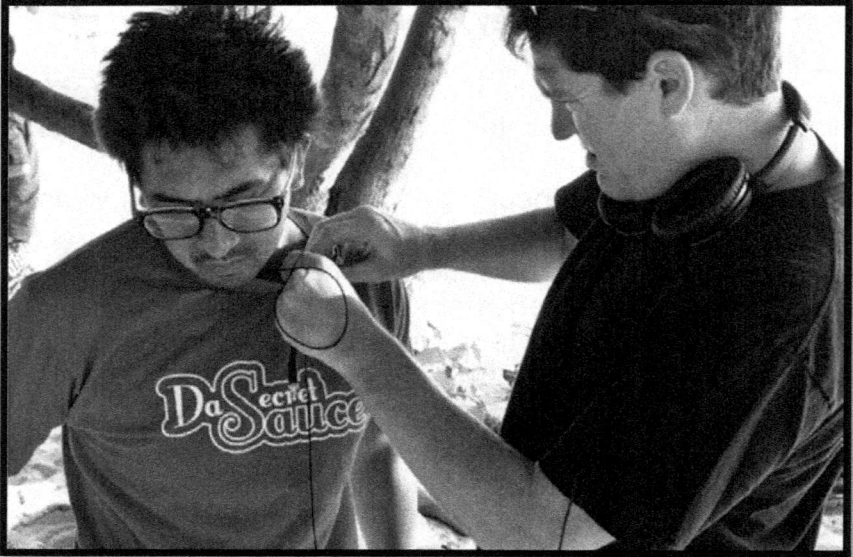

Rex Moribe (left) at work (shooting a TV pilot for the Food Network which didn't get picked up)...

...and at play

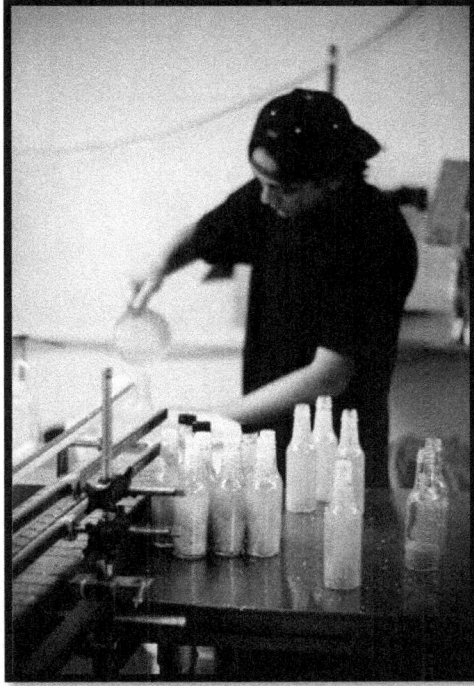

Rex's partner Jason Koji making the first batch of Da Secret Sauce

Lotsa bottles of chili water

Putting the label on

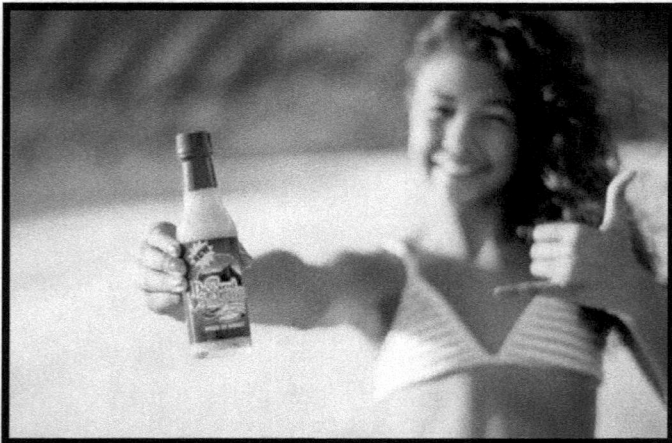
Enjoying the final product (Kaya Paterson showing Shaka)

Da Secret Sauce at work!

Da Secret Sauce product lineup

Chapter 5: Distilled Spirits
Haliimaile Distilling Company

HALIIMAILE
DISTILLING COMPANY

Makawao, Maui, HI
(808) 214 - 8801

haliimailedistilling.com
mark@levecke.com

Established
2008

Leadership
Mark Nigbur, Master Distiller

Products
Vodka, whiskey and rum

Creating Hawai'i in a bottle…

If you meet Mark Nigbur you very well might assume he was born in Hawai'i. He's got the look with his cascading blonde locks and laid-back, highly approachable attitude. In reality, Mark grew up, and spent most of his adult life in Colorado.

In fact, not only did he not grow up in Hawai'i, his career didn't begin in the distilled spirits industry either. The start of his adult life was spent in the Colorado-friendly industry of ice hockey. Mark owned and operated a hockey apparel and equipment company which catered to the NHL®.

In 2004 he was ready for a change. He had flown to the annual gathering where the teams purchased their equipment for the year right before rookie camps start. When it was announced the teams would be locked out, there was no market for his products. Insiders provided him with the information that the strike would be going on for a while (ultimately the entire season would be canceled).

Flying back to Colorado, Mark had a few vodkas on the plane. He was burnt out, ready to make a change, and with the strike he now had no customers. He knew right then he needed to make a big move with his career.

One of the articles in the United Airlines® in-flight magazine was about the proliferation of microbrewers starting up. While this grabbed Mark's attention, he wasn't interested in joining the growing legion of small companies producing beer. He wanted to be a distiller.

He thought he could improve upon the vodka he was drinking on the plane. In fact, he had a unique idea for distilling the vodka that included a glass still as opposed to the traditional copper typically utilized. He didn't have any experience in distilling, nor had he heard of anyone utilizing a glass still. He just believed it could work. He began to sketch out his ideas on a United Airlines® napkin.

Back in Colorado, the first thing Mark did was to find out if it was legal to open a distillery. He was pleased to find that there were no legal restrictions against him going into the business. He ended up receiving the second distillery license in the State of Colorado.

He then began working developing the glass stills he had designed. It took him six months, but the plan he had sketched out initially on the United Airlines® napkin actually worked. He had a working still made out of glass. This gave his company the look of a laboratory or operating room. He decided to call his vodka Altius which was Latin for highest which made sense since his distillery was at the highest altitude in the United States.

He, along with his friends and family, was pleased with his initial offering. As he began to sell it, customer feedback was extremely positive as well. Without his knowledge, a friend sent a bottle to the online blogger The Liquor Snob™. This was something Mark had considered but was worried about negative feedback so he had elected to not participate in online reviewers.

Mark was caught off guard when The Liquor Snob™ contacted him about their review. Not only were they extremely positive with their comments but they also elected to do an expanded review of his product. This positive feedback brought the attention of the family-owned LeVecke Corporation®, a rectifier and wholesale distributor of beer and wine.

They had been toying with the idea of opening a company in Hawai'i using pineapple to create vodka. They contacted Mark to see if he was interested in moving to Maui to run this business for them.

Mark had never been to Hawai'i, and with a wife and three children he was firmly established in Colorado. After a visit to Maui he was quickly convinced, it was the place for him. He closed his distillery, put his house up for sale and within 3 months had relocated to Hawai'i (his family would follow him about 2 months later).

He immediately began working on what would become his flagship product, Pau Vodka. The distillery was located on a pineapple farm. Utilizing the sugar from Maui Gold™ pineapples, he created the mash which would be used for his vodka.

Mark found the pineapple, a naturally fermenting fruit, to be perfect for utilization in vodka. The first distillation resulted in a product that was 97.5% clean. Though there isn't scientific data to back this up, Mark personally found the purity to translate to a product that was literally hangover free.

Unlike his initial trepidations with Altius, Mark, with the support of the LeVecke Corporation®, aggressively got the word out about Pau. The product immediately found an audience. In addition to distributors in Hawai'i, they also secured distribution in California, Texas, New York and Florida.

With a second hit on his hands, the industry began to take note of Mark and his efforts. His unique approach with the glass stills created a great deal of interest in the company, and it wasn't uncommon for individuals in the distilled spirits business to stop by when they were on vacation in Maui.

One such person was Steve Kauffman, the President of Cabo Wabo® tequila. Steve was not only impressed with the operation, but he took note of the fact that Mark looked a lot like Sammy Hagar, the owner of Cabo Wabo™. He told Mark he would have Sammy stop by to see what he was doing. Mark didn't know that Sammy had a house on Maui (that's where Steve Kauffman was staying) and spent a lot of time on the island.

The next time Sammy was in Maui, he did stop by Haliimaile Distilling. He had divested his stake in Cabo Wabo™ and was interested in a new opportunity. He asked Mark about whether he had considered making rum. Sammy had been interested in creating rum that captured the soul and spirit of Hawai'i. This seemed to be the perfect opportunity. After all, they had access to the highest quality cane sugar right there.

A partnership and friendship was formed on the spot. This wasn't a vanity project for Sammy either. Mark was pleased to find his hands-on approach to every facet of the business. From ingredients, to production and marketing, Sammy was involved in each step of what would become Sammy Hagar's Beach Bar Rum.

With children the same age, a joint interest in distilling and a love of Hawai'i, Mark and Sammy have become good friends. They often are together working on their rum, promoting it or just hanging out.

Today, business at Haliimaile couldn't be better. They are running the glass stills constantly with product heading out as soon as it is completed to meet demand. Currently, they are starting a remodel that will open up a tasting room and retail store onsite.

Sammy Hagar's Beach Bar Rum is available in all 50 states and sales continue to grow. Mark has also formulated two new products he is preparing to launch. Maui Moon Vodka is a flavored vodka line that will initially come in three flavors: Chocolate/Macadamia Nut, POG (a Hawaiian favorite, short for Passion Fruit/Orange/Guava) and Hibiscus. He has designed a tiki bottle for Maui Moon which should really make it stand out on store shelves.

His second new line is Paniolo Whiskey. Haliimaile Distilling is right in the middle of Hawaiian cowboy, or "paniolo", territory in what is known as the up-country portion of Maui. Paniolo Whiskey is a blended grain and pineapple whiskey. This represents a brand new category of whiskey so it should create quite a buzz. He is currently blending and aging it for a launch in 2014.

Mark couldn't be happier. He has a successful business and absolutely loves his life in Hawai'i. As he reflects back on his life in Colorado and the years of hustling to make ends meet selling his hockey equipment, he laughs. A cold winter day in Colorado likely meant snow and perhaps sub-zero temps in a stressful job working the phones and checking-in on accounts. Today, that winter day is probably in the mid-80's, he's in board shorts and a t-shirt. He's going to taste a few products, work the stills and perhaps give Sammy a call.

His only regret... why didn't he do this ten years earlier?

Haliimaile Distilling Company Photo Album

Mark Nigbur

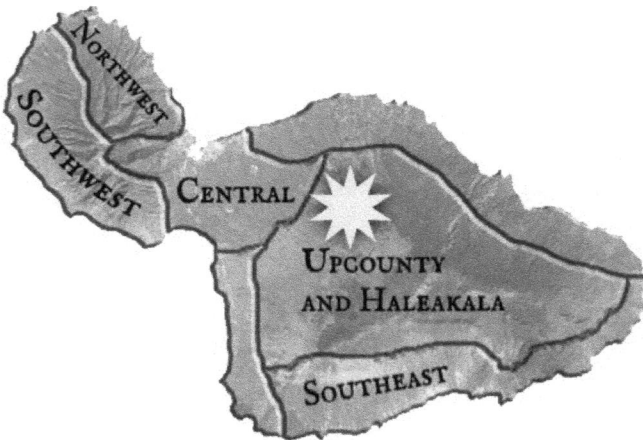

Haliimaile's location in Maui

Mark's glass stills give Haliimaile the feel of a laboratory

Mark talking distilling

Advertising for Pau Maui Vodka looks like your vacation photos

Mark making an appearance at a local liquor store

Mark showing off a bottle of Sammy's Beach Bar Rum

Cheers!

Chapter 6: Distilled Spirits
Island Distillers

Honolulu, O'ahu, HI
(808) 492-4632

islanddistillers.com
dave@islanddistillers.com

Established
2008

Leadership
Dave Flintstone, Proprietor

Products
Vodka, Coconut Vodka and Okolehao (traditional Hawaiian moonshine)

"I can't come to the phone right now, I am out of the office sourcing coconuts"...

As a young man, Dave Flintstone was determined to move to the island paradise of Hawai'i. To describe him as adventurous would clearly be an understatement when you consider as soon as he could get the cash together, he bought a one-way ticket and made the leap.

This was 1989 - long before you could put together a plan via the information available on the internet. This was literally one guy, a duffel bag, and nothing beyond. No plan. No friends or family to rely on. No contingency should things not work out.

He was a skilled bartender so he figured it would be relatively easy to find work in a tourist-based economy. He wasn't big into creature comforts so the local youth hostel served him perfectly for accommodations.

It turned out his lack of plan was perfectly fine. He did quickly find work. The youth hostel was great. Almost too perfect, really. Eventually they had to kick him out, reminding him it was a place to layover for traveling youths... not a permanent place to take up residence.

As he began to enjoy the beauty of Hawai'i, he became very active in scuba diving. Soon it transitioned from a hobby to a passion, and from there it continued to evolve to a source of income. Dave left his job as a bartender to become a scuba instructor.

When contacts got him hooked up with some scuba instructor gigs in the Caribbean, he began enjoying extended stays there. It was during the trips to the Caribbean that he discovered a favorite in the area: locally sourced rum. He found that these tiny island distilleries, with no shelf presence at all, were far superior to the product he had been serving over his many years as a bartender.

Dave began to develop some friendships which would lead him into internships with some of the distillers during his stays in the Caribbean. These were literally non-paying, but they offered him the opportunity to learn about distilling and the secrets of what made their products so superior to the big brands he was familiar with in the U.S.

By the mid-2000s he had grown a little weary of the unusual hours associated with tending bar and the unsteadiness of the work in scuba, so he began building houses and selling them. Business was going great until the real estate crash in 2007. With a market not conducive to selling homes, he decided to seek out this next adventure. In his mind it was very clear what he should do next. He wanted to call upon the skills he picked up in the Caribbean and get into the distilled spirits business.

For more than a year, he tried to get a distillery going in Maui. He found the red tape and government bureaucracy to be so difficult on the local level, he wasn't even able to get started. Without the local licensing and permits, he wasn't going to be able to secure the necessary federal approvals. All of this came together to mean there was no way he was starting this business in Maui. When he finally accepted the fact it wasn't going to happen, he decided to take one more shot at his dream by calling the regulators in O'ahu.

It's hard to say if it was more frustration or relief when you find out it took Dave one fifteen minute phone call to the powers-that-be in O'ahu to understand he wouldn't have any of the issues and challenges he was facing in Maui to get his business started in Honolulu. He immediately packed up and headed there to start his business.

Ease of licensing aside, he still faced more challenges to getting his business going. Dave wanted to bring the spirit of Hawai'i to his product. He had learned the business and was confident in his ability to get it going from a business perspective. He didn't want to follow conventional distilling methods, though. In his mind he had come up with a plan to create a crushed lava filtration system. On the Hawaiian Islands rain water flows naturally through lava and comes out clean and pure. He wanted to create a distillery utilizing this concept to smooth out his spirits.

It took him 3 ½ years to perfect, but in the end, Dave Flintstone was successful in creating the only crushed lava filtration distillery. He began by making vodka utilizing fermented sugar cane as the base. His next product was coconut vodka. While there wasn't a competitor at the time when he started, you can find coconut vodka on the shelves today. The difference with Dave's product, though, is he's using real coconuts to flavor his product, not artificial extracts and flavorings created in a lab somewhere.

You might be surprised to find out that there aren't any commercial coconut producers in Hawai'i. The trees are abundant on the Islands. In fact, they are closely associated with Hawaiian culture but there isn't any commercial farming of the product so Dave could buy his coconuts locally. Hence the need for an out-of-office message which has him sourcing coconut when he's in places like Thailand or the Philippines, preparing for a bottling of his coconut vodka.

His other product is Okolehao, or Hawaiian moonshine. This product is very different than the traditional moonshine you would find from a still in the woods. It's also not to be confused with the increasing popular un-aged whiskies you find on store shelves, often packaged in mason jars and labeled as moonshine.

Dave's Okoleahao is based on traditional Hawaiian distillation dating back 1790. Utilizing ti root and sugar cane, Dave has pieced together a recipe and process utilizing documentation from old Hawaiian newspapers. A highly literate culture, there were numerous local small newspapers in the native Hawaiian language. Searching for article on okoleahao and translating them, Dave was able to put together information about ingredients and processes that helped in him developing a recipe he is confident mimics the okoleahao which was distilled in large, round whale blubber pots. Translated, okoleahao means iron bottom, and the product made from this process took on the name from the pots it was distilled and cooled in which sat side-by-side. There is some dispute as to whether it began to be called "iron bottom" based on the fact the two rounded pots sitting next to each other looked like a large fanny or more of a literal translation as they did in fact have iron bottoms.

The end result of Dave's extensive research is a product which serves as a tribute to traditional Hawaiian culture and is different tasting than anything else you can find. The bottle itself is written in the traditional Hawaiian language and a neck hanger translates it to English.

After years of apprenticeships, trying to secure licensing and developing his own process, Dave finally was producing the products he had dreamt of making. Of course, he was only halfway there in terms of making it. He still had to get on store shelves. Hiring a distributor, he then became aware of the process it would take to actually make it on retailers' shelves. The process varies greatly by retailer. The first step is securing an appointment. The next step is to meet with the buyer (this often involves travel to the Mainland for Hawaiian-based companies as the retailers are mostly headquartered there). Once they approve a product, it isn't a matter of just placing it on the shelf. These shelves are carefully diagrammed and inclusion means waiting for the next time they are reset. This could mean a wait of more than six months. In total, it wasn't uncommon to anticipate a year-long wait to get on the shelves of a retailer, even if the local manager was interested in carrying the product.

The great news for Dave was that once it was on the shelves, his unique packaging has proven to garner the attention of potential buyers. It sells. He must have a good product as he is getting repeat business from buyers.

Dave has found stores very willing to try a locally-made product. Even the large chains are very interested in getting his locally-made goods on the shelves in their stores in Hawai'i, although it may involve the same long process to get them there.

Recently, Dave has looked to expand distribution to the Mainland. He has started to work with a distributor in California and is slowly gaining some footing into stores there. Should he achieve continued success, he will look to further expand outward across the U.S.

Dave is also looking to expand his business locally. His current Honolulu location is in an industrial area where he cannot offer tours, tastings or on-site purchases. He is currently seeking to move his business into a location wich would offer him all of that and much more.

Tours, tastings and on-site purchases allow customers to make a direct connection with the product and buy it right then. Dave also wants to move to expand his production capabilities. This would allow him to fully go after not only Mainland U.S. distribution, but international as well. The site Dave is seeking would also have room where he could grow local fruit and sugar cane. This would allow him to offer small batch products just to the customers visiting his distillery. This offers the potential for a unique experience which would not only be conducive to tourists, but locals seeking unique offerings.

For a guy who came to Hawai'i without a "plan," Dave has managed to do quite well for himself! After all, who else do you know that leaves an out-of-office messages stating they are sourcing coconuts?

Island Distillers Photo Album

Dave Flintstone (arghhhh!)

Non-pirate Dave at a store promotional event

The copper still at Island Distillers

Just a man and his vodka

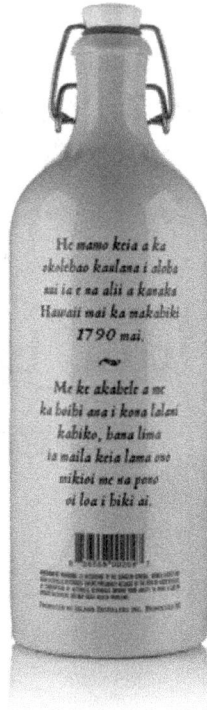

He mamo keia a ka
okolehao kaulana i aloha
nui ia e na alii a kanaka
Hawaii mai ka makahiki
1790 mai.

Me ke akahele a me
ka hoihi ana i kona lalani
kahiko, hana lima
ia maila keia lama ono
mikioi me na pono
oi loa i hiki ai.

The back of the Okoleahao bottle is written in the traditional Hawaiian language

Island Distillers product lineup

Chapter 7: Dog Treats
Maui Dog Treats

Wailea, Maui, HI
(808) 385 - 6202

mauidogtreats@gmail.com
dogtreatsmaui.com

Established
2013

Leadership
Heidi Cramer, Owner

Products
Healthy, all-natural dog treats in Peanut Butter Pumpkin and
Wheat Free Pumpkin flavors

Proving a healthy existence for our dogs is just as important for them as it is for ourselves…

From the time Heidi Cramer was a toddler, all she ever wanted to do was make dog treats. All-natural treats which she could not only market to dog lovers, but would also appeal to a tourist trade as well.

Just kidding.

It's unlikely anyone grows up thinking they are going to quickly build a business selling dog treats, but Heidi Cramer is living proof it can happen.

Like so many of the individuals profiled in the *Small Brand America* series, she grew up in a family surrounded by individuals who loved to cook. The passions of her mother and grandmother combined with the social aspects of the activity opened her up to the world of cooking early on.

The background in her family's cooking and baking still wasn't a precursor of Maui Dog Treats, the company she would open in 2013. That was going to involve a big move, several businesses with varying degrees of success and a beloved pet named Snoopy.

Heidi was raised in Los Angeles. At the age of 18, she took a job as a jewelry designer which facilitated a move to Santa Barbara. She worked for the company for a few years until she decided to go into business for herself, designing and selling costume jewelry.

By the time she was 27 she was burned out on the jewelry business. She saw an ad in the *L.A. Times* seeking individuals to work in the food service industry on the Island of Lana'i in Hawai'i. She decided to make the move with the goal of learning the restaurant business and saving up for culinary school.

She ended up working a variety of jobs: food and beverage manager, kitchen prep and assistant pastry chef. With Lana'i being so small, she sought further opportunities by moving to Maui.

While she didn't make it to culinary school, she did fully immerse herself into the food service by opening her own bakery, called Cakewalk, in 2000. She made a name for herself with the bakery by offering everything made from scratch onsite.

Business at Cakewalk was going really well until the economy started struggling in the mid – late 2000s. With costs for raw materials rising with increased fuel prices, it was not financially viable to continue her business. In 2008, after unsuccessfully searching for new owners, she closed her business.

When she began getting inquiries about selling wholesale, she opened back up only as a wholesale establishment (Cakewalk had been a retail bakery from 2000 – 2008). With a solid wholesale clientele, she was able to find a buyer for the company in 2010.

The new owner had great intentions of infusing cash into the company and growing the business. Heidi was even hired to run her former business for the new owners. The goals of a complete turnaround for the bakery never materialized, and it was closed for good in January of 2012.

After some time off, former customers began to contact Heidi about baking cakes for them. With a pent-up demand for her baking, she opened up a special events and wedding shop called Maui Sweet Cakes. This shop wouldn't feature retail/walk-up sales, but she would sell directly to consumers who needed event cakes in Hawai'i.

A special events bakery has highs-and-lows in demand. Heidi began to look at ways to level out her baking needs by offering a new product line.

She had been toying with the idea of creating a line of all-natural dog treats since 2008. Over the years she had started working on and testing recipes. She thought the focus on buying local and buying healthy for people might catch on for man's best friend as well. Having a retail line also would offer her the personal bonus of a steady stream of income which potentially could be more consistent than the world of event baking.

The inspiration for her business was Snoopy, her beloved mixed breed dog she got from the pound. Heidi had taken note of the various pet treat recalls over the years. Unlike the heavily regulated human food industry, pet food is largely unregulated. As such, the industry often struggles with health issues tied to inferior products.

After much research about what was healthy for dogs, and taste testing both with Snoopy and "friends of Snoopy," she developed two products: all-natural dog treats in Peanut Butter Pumpkin and Wheat Free Pumpkin flavors.

She then put together some human-eye attracting packaging, and Heidi had her Maui Dog Treats ready to sell. A lifetime in sales with both her jewelry company and then her own baking businesses prepared her to take her newest company to market. (She confidently notes, "Selling is the easy part.")

Just as she was getting going, tragedy struck when Snoopy developed cancer and died unexpectedly. Being that he was so important in providing inspiration, as well as built in test audience for her recipe development, it was a tough blow for Heidi. Rather than getting lost in grief, she continued to use Snoopy as an inspiration for her to continue to develop the brand. She couldn't help but feel had he been able to have healthier options like her dog treats throughout the course of his lifetime, perhaps he would still be here today.

One area Heidi hadn't prepared for success in was the tourism trade in Hawai'i. She started the business under the assumption she was creating a product designed to compete against traditional dog treats with a healthy alternative.

She quickly found individuals on vacation seemed to like the idea of picking up a souvenir for a family member who doesn't get to make the trip to Hawai'i, the dog.

In addition to her grocery and pet shop accounts, some of her biggest buyers have been hotels and gift shops. Heidi has even been able to further appeal to individuals buying souvenirs for the family pet by creating leis for dogs made of Maui Dog Treats. They make for a great photo opportunity when the family returns home, and then the string can be removed so the dog can enjoy a delicious (and healthy) treat.

Heidi is continuing to offer cakes through her Maui Sweet Cakes bakery. If you are getting married in Hawai'i, or having a party there, be sure to look her up: *mauisweetcakes.com*.

She is also planning to aggressively grow her Maui Dog Treats business. She is already in the process of expanding her distribution to other islands in Hawai'i. She has a few accounts on the Mainland but anticipates adding more there soon. She has interest in selling her treats in Germany right now and could see other countries following suit.

Heidi loves the fact there are individuals who have a passion about the health of their dogs. It's rewarding for her to know there are people who find her mission as important as she does.

With the quality of Heidi's product in an under-represented segment (healthy dog treats), and the selling skills she possesses, getting her product in a buyer's store is simply a matter of opportunity.

If she gets the chance to speak to them, she knows she'll have them sold!

Maui Dog Treats Photo Album

Heidi Cramer

Maui Dog Treats product detail

Snoopy – The inspiration for Maui Dog Treats

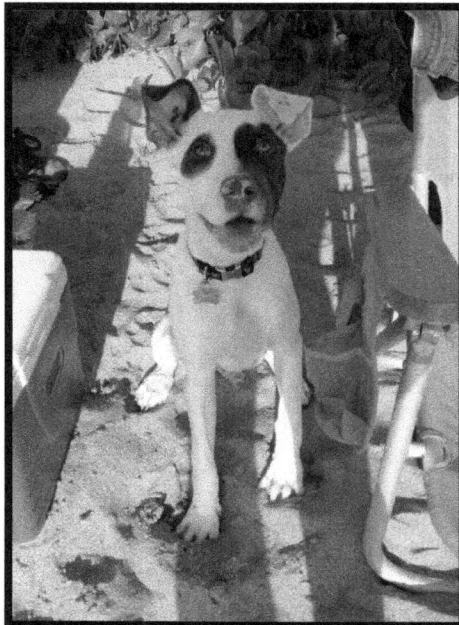

New Maui Dog Treats spokesdog, Simon

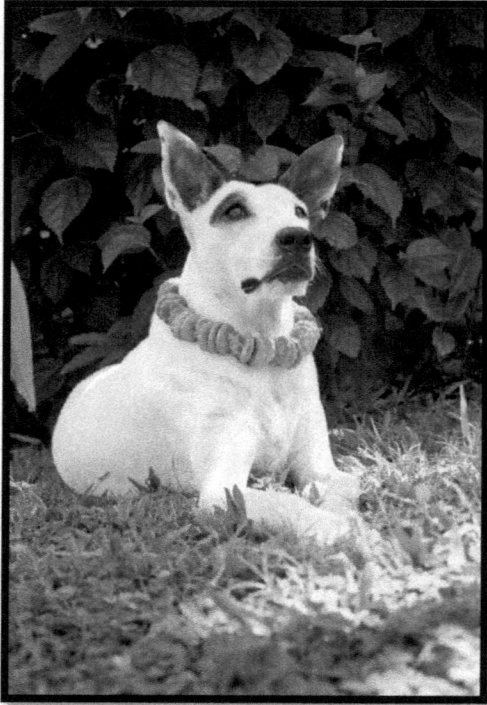

Vacation photo: check out the Maui Dog Treats lei!

Heidi and Snoopy chillin'

Maui Dog Treats packaging

Maui Dog Treats product lineup

Chapter 8: Goat's Milk Dairy Products
Surfing Goat Dairy

Surfing Goat Dairy
Maui Hawaii

3651 Omaopio Road
Kula, Maui, HI 96790
(808) 878 - 2870

surfinggoatdairy.com
info@surfinggoatdairy.com

Established
1999

Leadership
Thomas and Eva Kafsack, Owners

Products
Goat's milk cheese, truffles and soap

149 goats employed full-time...

For Thomas and Eva Kafsack, Maui was always a favorite vacation destination. Living in their native Hamburg, Germany, they used some of the proceeds from a partial sell-off of Thomas' software company to purchase a second home there in 1992. At that point, operating a successful dairy farm and tourist destination wasn't in their plans.

After completely selling his company in 1995, Thomas stayed on as a consultant through 1998 when they then wanted him to become CEO of the company he had once owned. While he was certainly qualified for the job, he wouldn't be the owner. He was hesitant to take a job where he would have to move to Frankfurt and report to mortgage bankers. When his doctor suggested taking the position might be detrimental to his long-term health, Thomas and Eva decided to make a move to Hawai'i and try something completely different.

One of the Kafsack's neighbors had been a goat farmer. Fresh goat cheese like they had at home in Germany, or even when they vacationed in France, was non-existent in Hawai'i. Their plan was a business far less stressful than running a software company. Their dream was to start a working goat farm with a bed and breakfast onsite in Maui.

In November of 1999, they found a 42-acre tract of land on Maui. Thomas thought it was the perfect spot for their goat farm and B&B. Eva wasn't so sure. She was staring at land covered in trash, rocks, dead trees and cactus.

Despite Eva's concerns, they purchased the property. It took them over two years to clear the land, get electric, install an underground irrigation system, acquire the necessary equipment for the farm, and build the buildings they would need to get started. The plan was to start the dairy farm and then add the bed and breakfast once they had the farm going.

Of course, up to this point they had been simply fans of goat cheese; they hadn't been farmers. In order to get started, they were going to have to learn the business from scratch. Eva took the lead on learning how to manage a goat farm while Thomas focused on overseeing the actual building of the farm.

Eva learned the business by jumping in with reckless abandon. In addition to spending time on the goat farm of their neighbor in Germany, she worked on farms in France and Austria as well.

In April of 2002, they were educated on the business, and the farm was ready to go. They got their final permits from the Health Department and opened for business. Their plan was still to open the B&B once they had income coming in from the goat farm.

It never happened, though.

No, it's not a sad story of lost opportunity. In fact, it's just the opposite. The farm was an instant success. After opening in April, by June they were already making inroads into local hotels and restaurants.

Before long, about 90% of all hotels on Maui and Waikiki carried their products. Double-digit growth each year for the business kept them so busy, they never had time to focus on getting the B&B going.

Despite all of the success, the Kafsacks managed to avoid having to use distributors and middlemen to get their product to market. They either personally delivered it or utilized overnight delivery to get their wholesale product in-stores. A model they continue to utilize to this day.

Additionally, Surfing Goat built up the farm as a tourist destination by offering tours. Visitors have three tour options:

Casual Tour – This 25-minute tour starts every thirty-minutes. Guests participate in an orientation on goat farming, they feed the goats and sample four kinds of cheeses.

Evening Tour – At 3:30 p.m. guests go on an extended tour which covers the duties of managing the farm. They then get to milk the goats and sample cheeses.

Grand Dairy Tour – On this Saturday-only tour, guests get to feed and milk the goats, see the cheese-making process, sample 20 cheeses from the dairy, and try a truffle.

Their 15,000 tours a year equates to over 60,000 guests enjoying a visit to Surfing Goat. This not only generates revenue for the farm, but also equates to direct sales to customers, many of whom become internet customers when they return home. About 2/3 of their revenue from selling the products made on the farm comes directly from sales to consumers who come to visit.

Surfing Goat has three main product lines (all made from fresh goat's milk):

1). Cheese – Their cheeses are divided into three categories:
- The Aloha line is soft cheeses made daily.
- The Paradise line is aged cheeses.
- The Shark Bite line (named for the "bite" they take out of your wallet) are specialty and luxury cheeses made from the finest ingredients (one even has 23k gold flakes in it).

2). Soap – 25 different scents including traditionals like lavender and lilac, tropicals like coconut and pineapple and local favorites like coffee beans or ginger lime.

3). Truffles – Goat's Milk Truffles is Surfing Goat's newest product line, but it has come on strong very quickly. The idea for getting into selling truffles is like a smaller version of opening the dairy itself. Eva and Thomas couldn't find truffles like they used to enjoy back in Europe.

They found their goat cheese to be a superior flavor enhancer for the truffles over the typical butter or heavy cream base found in most U.S. offerings. In fact, their taste is such an eye-opener, they found the first thing most guests trying a sample of their truffles said was, "Oh my" so they decided to name their product Oh My Truffles.

Currently, they offer 40 different varieties/flavors of their truffles. They are selling large volumes directly from the dairy as well as through hotels for conventions, large chain stores and through a unique partnership with Ocean Vodka®, which is made on a neighboring farm in Kula, Hawai'i. A notable high end retailer is currently in talks with Surfing Goat to carry their truffles nationwide.

The Kafsacks have also found a great way to give back with their Surfing Goat Dairy Farm. At any given time they likely have four or more apprentices on the farm. These individuals are often directed to them by the State Department, and they come from underdeveloped countries. They utilize the skills they learn at Surfing Goat to work on farms back in their home countries once their apprenticeships are complete.

They also work with ACT University and get a student apprentice for 3 months every year. These are students who are studying farming at the university. While farming isn't new to them, the notion of coming to a goat farm on a scenic strip of land on Maui tends to be very appealing for these young students. Thomas and Eva take great pride in helping these young farmers get their start and make a point of keeping up with them after they return home.

Their final "little piece of aloha" is they always are willing to help others out. Just like the assistance they needed to get started, Thomas and Eva often open up their farm to others wanting to learn the craft of goat farming. It's not unusual to find someone from New England, Alaska, New Mexico or just about anywhere else working on the farm to learn the trade.

While their children haven't expressed an interest in entering the business, Thomas and Eva plan to continue working on the farm for many more years. Their 3 ½ million dollar investment is worth over 8 million dollars today. Their goal is to continue to expand the business and eventually sell it to someone who would run it as a goat farm. They have no interest in selling out to someone who would turn their hard work into a subdivision.

The only downside, as busy as they are, it doesn't look like their bed and breakfast is getting built anytime soon!

Surfing Goat Dairy Photo Album

Thomas and Eva Kafsack

The stars of Surfing Goat Dairy

The fun theme of surfing goats carries throughout the farm

Plus, the goats actually "surf" there!

Hello!

Surfing Goat's newest edition: truffles

Surfing Goat Dairy's Goat's Milk Soap

Some of Surfing Goat Dairy's cheese lineup

Chapter 9: Gourmet Cooking Salts
Sea Salts of Hawaii

SEA SALTS OF HAWAI'I
GOURMET COOKING SALTS

Honolulu, O'ahu, HI
(808) 333-8211

seasaltsofhawaii.com
sandra@hawaiianislandstradingcompany.com

Established
2012

Leadership
Alexandra "Sandra" Gibson, Proprietor

Product(s)
Classic and flavored sea salts

A Hawaiian tradition where SALT is more than just "salt"...

Salt plays an important and highly visible role in Hawaiian culture. When something is new, whether it's a startup business, adventure or journey, it is typically given a traditional blessing which includes sprinkling of a unique pink-hued salt manufactured using age-old harvesting techniques. These salts are not sold, but can only be given as a gift by those who have access to them. When Sandra Gibson was looking to begin a new chapter of her life in Hawai'i, she looked to the island and its rich heritage to provide inspiration for her journey.

A life that crisscrossed the globe with deep ties to Hawai'i might not have seemed in the cards for Sandra when she was growing up. After all, she was born in Austria and hadn't planned to leave. While working at a U.S.-based hotel chain located in Austria, she met her future husband who was on a one-year assignment from the chain's Maui location.

When his year-long term was up, the two of them moved to Maui where Sandra went to work for Hawaiian Air®. Transfers back-and-forth between Hawai'i and the Mainland led to a few different careers including another job in the aviation industry and even ownership of a restaurant, but Sandra decided to carry out the dream of owning her own company when her husband was once again brought back to Hawai'i, this time in Honolulu in 2009.

Having an extensive business background, including being in the food service business via her restaurant, didn't begin to prepare Sandra for the undertaking of entering the food preparation and distribution industry. She began the arduous task of researching commercial food preparation and packaging laws.

Once she was comfortable entering the business, she began to research the viability of producing Hawaiian sea salts. Harvesting sea salt is a complex operation which involves a combination of equipment, knowledge and permission to do so (utilization of resources from the ocean is regulated so not everyone can simply just jump in and do this). Knowing Sandra and her company wouldn't be responsible on their own for harvesting the salt, Sandra needed to find the right company or companies to help her bring the base of her mixtures to market, meaning she had to go back to the research phase to find the right partner(s).

After expansive research and multiple meetings, she engaged two partners. One was based on The Big Island and the other Moloka'i. The two partners complemented each other for her business as both brought different specialties.

Sandra would utilize their harvested product as the base for her product offerings. She would then add in dehydrated ingredients to enhance or flavor them. Utilizing a simple system of trial-and-error, she began to experiment to formulate recipes which eventually would be the salts she would sell.

Finally, in 2012 her company was officially launched. Her product line included "Classics" which were salts with general and specific cooking uses. Additionally, incorporating traditional Hawaiian flavorings like pineapple, ginger and seaweed, she developed a line of "flavored" salts to go along with the flagship line of classics.

All were packaged in decorative tins or bottles with bold labels. This was done with great care by Sandra who wanted her product to not only appeal to those using it, but for the tourist trade as well. She felt like you couldn't get much better of a souvenir from Hawai'i than something as practical and fun as her salts.

Her products were great to look at (capturing the much needed shelf presence for the tourism trade), but they were highly suitable for capturing the essence of Hawai'i back home not only in cooking, but also with the tie-ins to culture and tradition.

The good news for Sandra was the tourism industry took note. With her personally making the calls, she soon began partnering with local shops. Next, there were hotels and then big companies like Disney®, Dole® and even the famous Hawaiian tour stop of Hilo Hattie's® were onboard with Hawaiian Sea Salts.

Not only is Sandra making incredible inroads in establishing her product, from day one of operation she has taken a socially conscious approach as well. She utilizes an agency which assists mentally disabled adults by providing them employment for some of the work she does in preparation and packaging.

Additionally, she earmarked one-percent of all wholesale and retail sales to go directly to a charitable fund she created to benefit the Papahānaumokuākea National Marine Sanctuary. This is not only the longest named conservation site, it is also the largest conservation area in the United States.

This federally protected area became a national monument in 2006. It covers an area roughly 140,000 square miles of marine habitat and is home to the largest predator-dominated coral ecosystem in the world. For comparison, Yellowstone National Park covers 3,468 square miles of land.

Despite the fact there is no commercial or private fishing allowed in the sanctuary, tons of debris floats in every day. This poses serious threats to not only the underwater marine life which gets trapped in the netting or killed from eating it, but the birds as well. Large birds like the Albatross eat the plastic which washes in, and their bodies cannot digest it so it ends up filling their stomachs, and they literally starve to death with a stomach full of manmade debris. Sandra's donations help in assisting the sanctuary in removing this harmful debris. It's just her own way of giving back to the ocean for what it is giving her company.

If her business continues to grow at the trajectory it has in its first year, it appears Papahānaumokuākea National Marine

Sanctuary is going to be getting a considerable amount of support from Sandra and her Hawaiian Sea Salts Company. She not only continues to grow her business in the retail and hotel segments, she is also beginning to make inroads with event planners in the hospitality sector. She has begun to cater to trade shows and other types of events with guest coming to Hawai'i. She has also dovetailed off of this concept by approaching companies to offer her product to customers, visiting dignitaries or employees. Just like in the tourist trade, she has found her packaged salts make the perfect take home memory of the event and the Hawaiian Islands.

A typical day for Sandra can vary widely as she continues to be involved in every facet of her business. Whether it's planning, production, marketing, product delivery or sales calls, Sandra is involved, making critical decisions for her brand.

It appears she has potentially large opportunities ahead of her as well. She is currently in discussions with two distributors to begin carrying her product in Japan. She also continues to assess the market for the U.S. Mainland. Developing a distribution strategy that makes sense financially has been challenging, but she continues to keep the door open to expand distribution there, too.

There is a lot which goes into building a successful company. A great product is always the foundation, but you also need capital, good timing and perhaps a little luck along the way. Thus far, Sandra has managed to deliver on all of those tangents with Hawaiian Sea Salt. Of course, she may have another factor working for her.

When she started her business, she elected to have a traditional Hawaiian blessing from a Kumu (teacher) who was able to utilize salt from Ni'ihau, "The Forbidden Isle." Ni'ihau is inhabited only by native Hawaiians and has very little tourism.

Not only was her company blessed with this sacred and unique salt, she received a small gift of the excess. This special salt can be procured by very few and is extremely rare. Susan keeps her gift on her desk as a reminder to the ties her company has to the history and culture of Hawai'i.

It appears as though her secret weapon is working well!

Sea Salts of Hawai'i Photo Album

Sandra Gibson

Sea Salts of Hawai'i's products capture the spirit, traditions and the culture of the Hawaiian Islands

Sampling station featuring the canned product

Sampling station featuring the bottled product

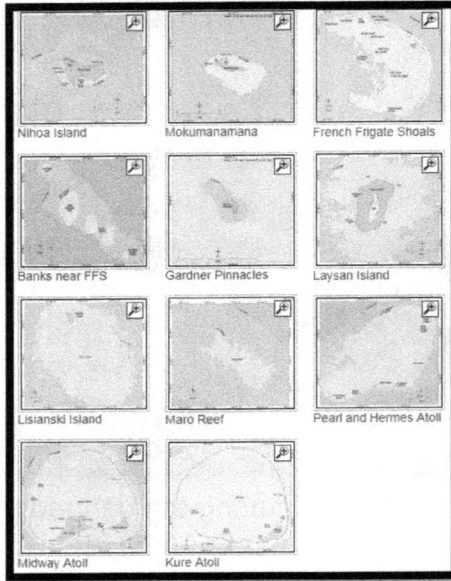

Nihoa Island	Mokumanamana	French Frigate Shoals
Banks near FFS	Gardner Pinnacles	Laysan Island
Lisianski Island	Maro Reef	Pearl and Hermes Atoll
Midway Atoll	Kure Atoll	

One-percent of Sea Salts of Hawai'i's sales go to benefit the
Papahānaumokuākea National Marine Sanctuary

Sharks at the sanctuary

Gift basket of bottled product

Gift basket of the canned product

Chapter 10: Fresh Juice
Akamai Juice Company

Kilauea, Kaua'i, Hawai'i
(808) 639 - 3513

akamaijuice.com
akamaikauai@gmail.com

Established
2009

Leadership
Cas Schwabe, Owner

Products
Fresh juices (and the coolest hats... ever!)

Introducing kids to vegetables, one glass of juice at a time...

Meet Cas Schwabe.

She is the actress, producer, photographer, personal assistant, music industry cook, caterer, celebrity personal chef, former sporting goods store owner, indoor skate park designer, former women's high fashion store owner and Kaua'i's first female helicopter pilot who owns and operates the Akamai Juice Company.

It has been a well-traveled journey to get to own her juice company, but it all started in Charleston, West Virginia where she was born. She went to high school in Maryland and college in Virginia. It was during her college years where she got her introduction to the film industry.

The mini-series, *A Woman Named Jackie* was filmed near her college campus. She decided to get involved and ended up landing a job as an assistant to Roma Downey, the lead actress in the production. She enjoyed being part of the production and made some excellent contacts along the way. She also struck a friendship with the caterer. Between the on-set production contacts and the catering company, Cas had established friendships which would allow her to continue to pursue a career in the entertainment industry.

For the next twenty years she would drift in and out of the movie, television and music industries. Personal relationships, or the need for work/money, would draw her back. Between stints in entertainment-related fields, she would work at home in West Virginia. For a period, she ran Schwabe-May, a high-end women's fashion clothier started by her family in 1880 in Charleston.

Another business she owned was a sporting goods store. Realizing she was paying rent on a basement she couldn't utilize as retail space, she decided to put it to use by designing an indoor skate park. The idea was to bring potential customers to the store by offering a form of entertainment which wasn't available anywhere else in West Virginia at the time. In the end, it proved to be more of a free babysitting service, but it was exciting bringing something brand new to the area.

Over time, Cas had developed a fondness for the juice blends available on the sets of the movies on which she was working. She was on the catering side herself at times. There she got to learn about the creation of flavor pairings as well as the healthful benefits of these tasty blends. She had even gained the trust of some of the celebrities she met on set where she would work as their personal chefs during production.

In 2004, working in the catering side of the film industry, she decided she needed a change. She was ready for something completely different. A friend had moved to the island of Kaua'i in Hawai'i and had an extra bed available.

Knowing she would have low overheard with the living arrangements, and flush with cash ("pimp stacks" as Cas referred to them) from working in the entertainment industry, she decided to try her hand at living another dream. She had always wanted to be a helicopter pilot, and there is a fairly decent-sized need for pilots in Kaua'i.

Cas had moved to Kaua'i at a time when the economy was struggling. Helicopter flight lessons cost $250 an hour. Securing the multi-tiers of licensing needed to be a pilot requires many hours of training as well as ongoing lessons. As the economy improved, the cost of the lessons began to rapidly increase. Soon, the price jumped to $750 an hour.

Cas knew she needed a supplemental form of income to be able to continue to live in Hawai'i. She had a lot of experience in the food business through her work as a caterer and a personal chef. Plus, her entire family had always been obsessed with the food and beverage industries. Her step-father had been in the restaurant business so she felt she had a well-rounded sense of trying to make a go of a business in the food industry.

Her idea for a business was to break away from the conventional recipes, an approach her family had used in their businesses. Her goal was to utilize the fresh fruits readily available in Hawai'i to create a juice business. She had seen so many unique pairings on the sets of movies, she thought she could refine what she knew and offer something pretty special which would be truly uniquely Hawaiian. She started off just making juice for herself and friends. It was a hit so she looked to officially expand into a juice company.

She chose the name Akamai to call her business which is the Hawaiian word for "smart or clever." Her plan was to create fresh juice utilizing local, organic, raw and natural ingredients and only what was in-season. She wanted to offer the freshest product possible. Cas wasn't interested in offering a packaged product through grocery stores. Akamai was to be a juice bought and served fresh.

Her distribution plan was three-pronged:
1). Sell directly to customers at the local farmers' market
2). Sell to accounts (hotels/restaurants) looking to serve freshly made Hawaiian juices to its customers
3). Offer in-home delivery to customers who wanted the product brought to them.

Her planning has worked because this is exactly what Cas has been able to deliver. She is a regular at the Saturday Hanalei Farmers' market where she gets to provides samples and interacts with past, present and future customers. This hands-on approach helps her increase the word-of-mouth buzz (humorously called "coconut wireless" in Hawai'i) she needs to continue to grow her business.

Many of the customers met at the Hanalei Market turn into home delivery customers. This means fresh juice would be brought directly to their homes. As a small business owner, it is often Cas making the deliveries as well as the juice.

She also has numerous restaurants and hotels on Kaua'i which have also started serving Akamai Fresh Juice to their patrons, who are looking for a true "taste of Hawai'i" while visiting.

Over time, Cas has developed really strong relationships with local farmers, which allow her to have plenty of the freshest ingredients on-hand at all times. She is at the point now when they have bruised fruit (perfect for juicing), they call her. Having a source for ingredients is important because business is booming. During busy times, Cas can be "juicing" seven days a week to keep up with demand.

She is usually fully immersed in her business unless one of her old celebrity pals calls. While she is out of the entertainment industry (at least for now), if one of her old buddies like Woody Harrelson or Matthew McConaughey call looking for a personal chef during a shoot, she's usually more than willing to help out.

Her celebrity connections have proven solid for business in a variety of ways. Many of her pals have taken a liking to the custom designed "trucker hats" she has made by local artist Maxine Graham to promote her company. One of her music industry pals was Red Hot Chili Peppers singer Anthony Kiedis. Cas cooks for him when he stays on the island. During one of his stays on Kaua'i, he bought some of her unique and colorful Akamai Juice hats.

While she noticed he was always wearing his Akamai Juice Company hats around her during his vacations, she didn't realize he was wearing them all over the globe until Red Hot Chili Pepper fans began contacting her. They wanted hats like the frontman of their favorite band was wearing (RHCP guitarist Josh Klinhoffer also has bought some of the hats). Soon, it became a fun connection with Chili Pepper fans, sharing photos of Anthony wearing his hats all over the world. He now has a tradition of buying six hats for himself and his son every time he visits. Cas' Facebook® page has almost become a "Where's Anthony" as she shares the latest Kiedis/Akamai hat sighting.

Her Facebook® page is also a way to interact with fans of her juice. She's been known to ask what flavor pairing customers have come across in their travels. When cucumber/mint came in as a suggestion, she worked to make it her own by also pairing some Hawaiian flavors like pineapple, coconut, ginger and turmeric.

One of her most popular combination is one she calls Magic Dragon (her #1 seller is her Cucumber Mint Slushy). To give you an idea of the complexity of her flavor profiles, here's a look at what goes into her Magic Dragon offering (all ingredients are local and organic): aloe, avocado, apple banana, basil, beet greens, bok choy, cilantro, collards, cucumber, kale, lime, Ni'Oi Chili, parsley, pineapple, Swiss chard and turmeric. As you can see, this business isn't just someone with a food processor and a bag of produce. She has taken an artisanal approach to her creations.

With a rapidly expanding direct client base and several large corporate clients in the works, it appears Akamai Fresh Juice will continue to grow on the creativity of Cas Schwabe. Unless, of course, Cas decides she wants to be a thermonuclear physicist. If she does, she will undoubtedly be successful in that field as well.

Thus far, it appears Cas can do whatever she sets her mind to!

Akamai Fresh Juice Photo Album

Cas Schwabe

Fresh juice on ice

Cas' friends include the equine types (pictured here with her 11-year-old Arabian Sunny)…

…and celebrities like Matthew McConaughey

The famous Akamai Juice Company hats designed by local artist Maxine Graham

Akamai's fans often send Cas photos of Anthony Kiedis out and about in the Akamai Juice hats

Cas showing off her other passion: flying a helicopter

Akamai Juice Company product lineup

Chapter 11: Fresh Juice
Govinda's Fresh Juices

521 Kuwili Street
Honolulu, O'ahu, HI 96817
(808) 533-3621

govindasjuice.com
govindas@govindasjuice.com

Established
1982

Leadership
Jim Eichler, CEO

Products
Fresh juices

Govinda Defined: One who gives pleasure to the senses…

How do you parlay a small cookie business into a juice company that can hold its own against the likes of such megabrands as Pepsi®, Campbells®, Welch's® and Coca-Cola® with not a lot more to support you than an admitted "so-so" website?

Well, that would be the story of Jim Eichler.

It actually kind of starts out more as an "after school special" than the tale of a tycoon. It seems Jim was a bit, let's say unfocused, as a young man. He had a job as a beer salesperson in New York City. When the company made some cuts, he was laid off.

It was 1977 and 22-year-old Jim decided he needed a change. He had been a bit rebellious and was simply tired of living in New York. He really wanted to go to a place which was a little more laid back. Some place he could spend his days surfing.

Where better than Hawai'i?

Since he was collecting unemployment, he inquired if he could transfer his benefits to Hawai'i. When he was told he could, it was the affirmation he needed to make the change. He packed a suitcase, a surfboard, and flew to O'ahu.

For a guy who is now so focused on his business (literally a visionary who gets involved in every aspect of running his company), it seems hard to believe he wouldn't have a plan for a move as big as this, but he didn't. He didn't know anyone in Hawai'i. He had no job prospects. He actually had no idea where he would be staying. He just knew one thing: he wanted to surf.

Upon landing in O'ahu, he made a beeline to the North Shore, the Mecca of surfing. Like so many of those "after school special" stories, he met some new friends who were able to help him out with the basics: food and shelter. After plenty of time enjoying the adventures of his new home and with his unemployment benefits running out, Jim began to look to what he could do to support himself. Rather than continuing to work for someone else, he thought it might be a good time to go the entrepreneurial route. His idea was to bake cookies and sell them to convenience stores and gas stations for on-premise purchase. This was before offering fresh baked cookies at these types of establishments was commonplace.

Initially, the cookie business was really strong. He was baking them himself at his home and then delivering them to accounts he had established. The cookie business had the potential to be the end of the story for Jim, but when national brands began to offer fresh-baked cookies for on-premise purchase, he decided to look to something else.

One segment which had captured his attention was fresh juice. There was a health food store he frequented where they would make fresh carrot juice right in the store. He had always wondered why someone didn't make these types of juices, bottle them and make them more widely available beyond health food stores. After all, fresh juice was not only delicious, but also he had been reading up on all of the health benefits.

He decided to jump in and start a juice company. Drawing upon some of the Eastern Philosophy he had studied, he named the company Govinda's Fresh Juice. He liked the fact it was loosely defined as "one who gives pleasures to the senses" as well as the idea that there is a Hindu God with the name Govinda.

Purchasing some small equipment and pressing the juice in small batches, he established the business in 1982. At the time, he really didn't have any competitors and found it easy to get his unique blends on the shelves of health food stores, grocery stores and hotels and restaurants which were seeking to offer its customers true fresh juice.

When competition did begin to pop up, Govinda didn't have any problems fending them off if customers did a taste test. His "hand-squeezed/small output" approach meant he had superior flavor. This literally came as a direct result of juicing only the fruit. Larger companies with their large machinery are going to "juice" the peel as well as the fruit. This is not only a quicker approach; it extends the output from the fruit. The downside is the oils from the peel negatively change the flavor profile. The juice takes on a slightly bitter taste and doesn't taste like a bite of fresh fruit.

Utilizing this approach, Jim managed to consistently grow his business until a big change in 2004 made him evaluate how he did business. Prior to 2004, juice wasn't required to be pasteurized. This was an offshoot of the fact the acidity of the fruit meant it was very low risk for harmful pathogens. This all changed when a competitor's product ended up having harmful pathogens and a two-year old died. The FDA stepped in and announced all juice products, other than citrus juices, would need to be pasteurized from that point forward.

Controversy surrounded this decision. There was talk that it may have been driven by the megabrands to add a process which would make it difficult for the small brands to adhere to. Once again, Jim saw it as an opportunity to differentiate his company from the larger brands.

There is a secondary approved process to ensure juices are pathogen safe. It was a little more time consuming, and, yes, more expensive. The process, using Ultraviolet (U.V.) lighting, provides the same protection as the heating process of pasteurization. The upside to the U.V. approach is there isn't the loss of vitamins, enzymes and taste. While it meant that Jim once again was facing a higher production cost, it also meant he was offering the same level of quality and taste his fans had come to expect from his company.

Jim has also been a bit of a contrarian when it comes to the trends. When something gets hot, the acai berry for instance, all competitors offer it. Jim stays away from the new "it" flavors and trends. He looks for holes in the market: juice flavors not being offered by competitors. One he recently introduced, Ginger Rush (ginger/lemon-lime) has been a big hit and is currently one of his best sellers. He attributes this to the fact it's different than anything anyone else has out there. If he had introduced Govinda Acai instead of Ginger Rush, he doesn't doubt there would be some demand for it, but simply not the level he has experienced with his product which is totally unique to the market.

Using the core philosophies of offering unique small batch products without a process that diminishes the taste and health benefits has been very good for Jim and Govinda. He's been able to continue to grow his business even with tough economic times and an onslaught of new competitors. He tried advertising but saw no increase in demand so he stopped. He built his website himself and while he knows it could be much better, he's always amazed at how he connects to individuals and fans of his products through the site.

In fact, the only negative thing he can point out over the time he's owned Govinda made him a better company. When Starbucks® came to the market, they contacted him about being in their stores. They stated they were the best coffee, and they wanted the best fresh juice in their stores. They had sampled everything on the market, and his product was what they wanted represented in Starbucks®. As you can imagine, for a small company this was an incredible opportunity. His product was quickly offered in all of the Hawaiian Starbucks® stores, and it was selling well. One day the Starbucks® team showed up unannounced to perform a quality audit. Not having worked with a company like Starbucks® before, he told them what he did in terms of process. They wanted it documented in writing. Even though he was doing all of the right things, without written documentation, he failed the audit which led to the removal of his product from the stores.

Jim took this as a learning opportunity. Immediately, he began a process of documenting his procedures which are now standard requirements working for large companies. He is pleased to note how well it has paid off for him. His approach has helped him land more opportunities with larger retailers. Recently, he had an audit from Costco®, and he was pleased to note he scored 100 on that audit.

Jim couldn't be happier where he is right now. His brother Tom has moved from New York to join him, and it has really been helpful for him. Tom oversees the production side of the business. Jim continues to get involved in a little bit of everything: product development, sales, marketing, finance; he even fixes the machines.

The company has evolved from hand-pressing their juices to a modern facility which now replicates their hand-pressed approach. One of their competitors with nation-wide distribution sent their management team for a tour of Govinda's (they were a friendly competitor prior to being bought out by a large multi-national conglomerate). Despite their market share and resource advantages, their competitor couldn't believe how far ahead of them Govinda's was in terms of their facility.

All of the big name resort hotels (Sheraton®, Marriott®, Four Seasons®, Hilton®, Hyatt®, Ritz Carlton® and many more) feature Govinda's as their house juices. They also seem to have a lock on Hawai'i's thriving local film industry. Govinda's has a list of films/TV shows in which its juices are offered on-set including all of the following: *Hawaii Five-O*, *Pirates of the Caribbean*, *Lost*, *Battleship* and the new ABC® show *Off the Map*.

Jim Eichler's "pie in the sky" idea for the business could be a factory and distribution on the Mainland in the U.S. Then again, he'd probably be just as happy doing what he he's doing right at home in Hawai'i.

Not too bad for a guy who showed up with a suitcase, surfboard and an unemployment check!

Jim Eichler

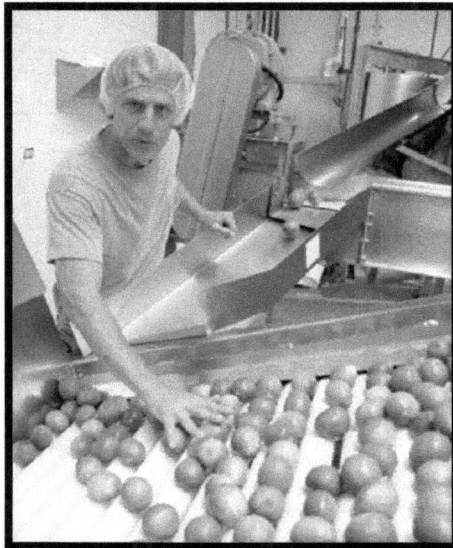

Jim's brother Tom has joined the company to help on the production side.

Soon to be juice!

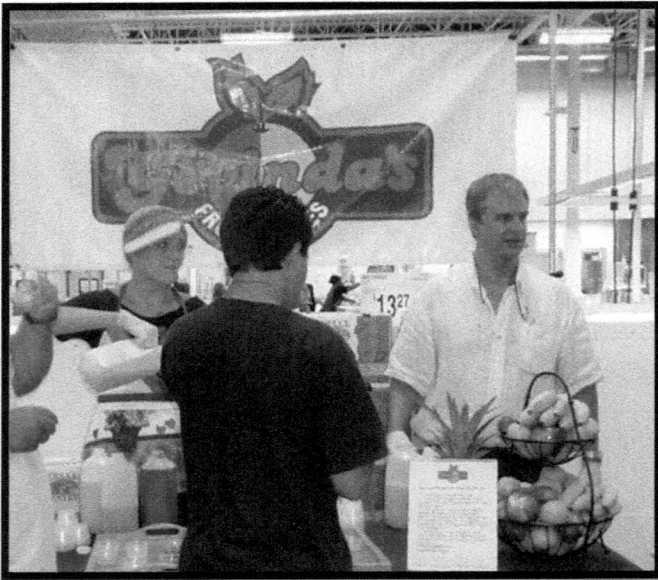
Meeting customers at an in-store demo

A look at the detail of Govinda's label

Govinda's product line-up

Chapter 12: Granola
Anahola Granola

3567 Hanapepe Road
Hanapepe, Kaua'i, HI 96716
(808) 335 - 5240

anaholagranola.com
info@anaholagranola.com

Established
1986

Leadership
Becky Burns, Owner

Products
Granola, trail mix and granola bars

A story of product without compromise when it comes to quality ingredients, personal perseverance and a lucky suit…

Becky Burns was born and raised in Seattle. Summers were spent on the nearby Orcas Island (part of the San Juan Islands between the state of Washington and Vancouver Island, British Columbia).

Her great-grandfather was very well-known in and around Seattle. He actually was the mayor there at one point. He and Becky's great-grandmother had a home on Orcas Island, and she considers the time during those summers even more important in the development of who she is than the time spent the rest of the year at home in Seattle.

After graduating high school, Becky went to college on the East Coast. Her first foray into entrepreneurialism occurred when she was at college. She started a cake business, marketing to the parents of the girls there. For birthdays, and other celebrations, cakes could be ordered through her. She then outsourced the baking to a local baker.

The money she earned selling cakes her freshman year was enough for a one-way ticket to Hawai'i. While she had visited there on family vacations, her real interest in visiting came from her college roommate who lived there. Becky planned to spend the summer vacation visiting with her roommate. In 1969, as soon as school let out, she got on a plane and headed to Honolulu.

Needing to earn money for her return trip, she got a summer job on the graveyard shift at Dole®, trimming pineapples. As the youngest member of the crew, and the only non-local, she was subjected to plenty of practical jokes and good-natured ribbing. She saved enough of her salary of just over a dollar-an-hour for the return ticket back to school in the fall.

After graduation from college, she moved back to the West Coast. She took a job as a caretaker on a private island, living by herself in a one-room log cabin on one of the San Juan Islands. It was there, in 1972, where she cooked up her first batch of granola on the stove of her cabin.

She wasn't ready to go into the granola business just yet... in fact, she hadn't even considered granola as a future business. It was just a tasty, and healthy, treat to enjoy and was easy for her to prepare with her limited resources at the time.

She then took a job at a shelter working with people with mental disabilities. She started an organic garden there and noticed a significant improvement in the quality of life for the people. They enjoyed the work and the fact they could make their own money growing and selling the produce they grew to local restaurants.

After leaving the shelter she completed her degree in Honolulu and then lived for a year on Moloka'i. She then decided to make what would be a life-change . She moved to Kaua'i, and it just felt different to her than any place she had been. Frankly, it just felt like home.

Since her first experiment with granola on her caretaker job, Becky had continued to make granola. Often she would give it to friends, family and neighbors. They always told her she needed to open up a granola business.

She never really considered it seriously until Christmas of 1986. She was a single mother with a 2-year-old daughter. She thought a hobby business of selling granola might be a nice secondary income. Kaua'i has a holiday fair every Christmas. Becky packaged up her product and hand-labeled them for sale at that year's fair.

To her amazement, she not only sold out, she made a great contact with a woman who owned a local store. She told Becky that if she could produce her granola commercially, she would be her first corporate customer.

Becky drew upon her past experiences to officially launch Anahola Granola. There was a community kitchen in a facility for individuals with mental disabilities. She was able to utilize the staff there to make her granola. Once again she was able to find a way to create a positive environment and employment for individuals with mental disabilities.

Once she began producing her product, she needed to secure accounts to sell her granola. Being a single mother with limited resources, she relied on what she would refer to as her "lucky suit."

When she would secure an appointment with a potential customer, she would put on her one good business suit and bring in some samples. Of course, it was the granola itself which was getting her all of those new customers, but still, who is going to break a good luck streak? Even when income started rolling in from her new accounts, Becky had to wear the lucky suit when she was really going after a new customer.

With no employees, once she secured an account, it was up to her to deliver the product. It became a familiar sight to see her young daughter Malia strapped in a car seat in the car with Becky as she made her local deliveries.

It really looked like she had something going when Hurricane Iniki devastated the island of Kaua'i. The wrath of Iniki resulted in large scale damage to much of the island. With residents struggling to simply survive, and the tourism non-existent, Anahola Granola quickly lost the momentum Becky had built up.

When Becky was ready to get back to her business, Kaua'i wasn't quite ready for her. Much of the island still didn't have electricity. Becky loaded up samples and began to travel to O'ahu, The Big Island and Maui. She found the hotels, resorts and stores there to be very receptive to and supportive of a struggling business owner from Kaua'i.

Once she got electricity back, she had a whole new list of customers. Becky proudly notes that today, over 20 years later, these are still some of the strongest business relationships she has, and they remain some of her best customers.

Over the years, Becky has expanded her product line. Her initial offering was a granola with walnuts. She then added a tropical version which included macadamia nuts, papaya and pineapple. She also now has a mango-ginger granola.

Additionally, she has added trail mix and granola bars she calls MacaMania Bars to her product line-up as well. The bars were the most difficult to create. It was a challenge to get the recipe right for a chewy bar which didn't fall apart.

In 2006, she made a huge move to significantly ramp-up her business. She bought a building which would serve as the manufacturing, warehouse and distribution facility for Anahola Granola.

Currently, business for Anahola Granola is stronger than ever. She has distribution with distributors on the Hawaiian Islands, a few accounts on the Mainland and even a distributor in Japan.

Her daughter Malia, just two years old when Becky started the business, is an adult living in Chicago. She went to school in Seattle to get an education/teaching degree. She is now the Dean of Students for a school in Chicago.

Malia literally grew up in the granola business helping her mom with various tasks over the years. Even today, from her home over 4,000 miles away, she continues to help her mom. She provides help with packaging design, marketing and social media.

Currently, Becky has a team, which is like an extended family for her, who help run and manage Anahola Granola. She has bakers who have been with her for over 10 years so she doesn't have to get involved in the day-to-day tasks of baking the granola like she did when she started the business.

She states the most rewarding part of running her company is the fact she is introducing people to healthy foods which are tasty. She hopes her business will go on forever. Nothing makes her feel happier than the thought of people always being able to buy Anahola Granola.

Anahola Granola doesn't have a hall of fame at its corporate headquarters in Hanapepe, Hawai'i. If they did, the opening exhibit would likely be the lucky suit Becky sported during those early years.

Of course, when your product is as good as Anahola Granola, you really don't need a lot of luck. In actuality, all you need is someone with passion, perseverance, determination and a vision to get the product to market.

Someone like Becky Burns.

Anahola Granola Photo Album

Becky Burns

Becky and Malia Burns, then and now

The bakery crew at Anahola Granola

A look at the local landscape on Kaua'i

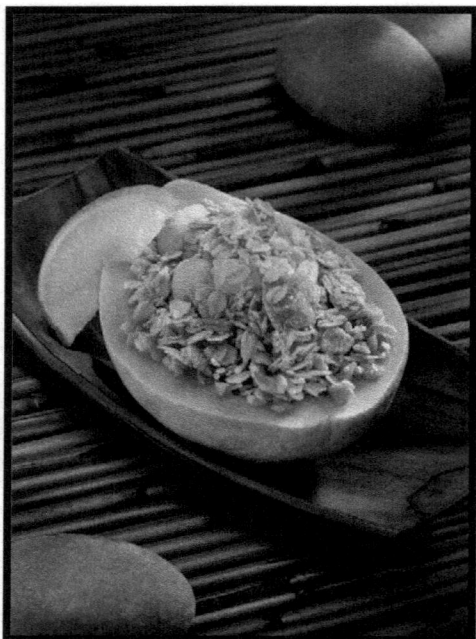

Granola & papaya: a healthy choice

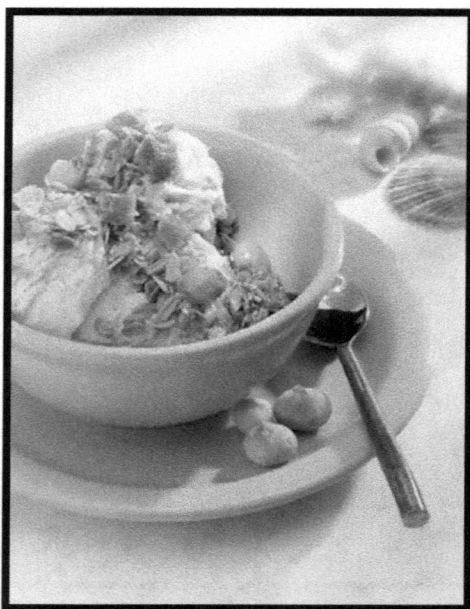

Granola & ice cream: a fun choice

Anahola's newest product is granola bars

Anahola Granola product lineup

Chapter 13: Honey

Moloka'i Meli, LLC

Made in Hawaii by

MOLOKAI MELI

Naturally produced under organic apiary practices.

Moloka'i, Hawai'i
(800) 434 - 2550

realhawaiiahoney.com
molokaimeli@gmail.com

Established
2004

Leadership
Brenda and Dennis "Denny" Kaneshiro, Managing Partners

Products
Kiawe honey

To God BEE the glory…

Brenda and Denny Kaneshiro first met through a mutual friend and were married in 1991. Both were living in O'ahu at the time… Denny having grown up there and Brenda having moved from her native Oregon (she had spent a portion of her childhood in Hawai'i and longed to move back so she did as soon as she was an adult).

After getting married and having two children (with the third of their eventual four children on the way), they moved to Moloka'i. They liked the idea of the more rural, less crowded environment of Moloka'i. Denny was working as a nutritional consultant, and Brenda was a stay-at-home mom who homeschooled their children.

When the owner of the nutrition consulting firm decided Moloka'i was too remote for him, he closed the business and moved away. Denny was left with a growing family and no job. With only one casual acquaintance on the island, Brenda and Denny felt like outsiders in a very tight-knit community. To survive, Denny began to take a series of odd jobs. He worked on a ginger farm, in construction and driving a rubbish truck. These weren't jobs he had an interest in as a career, but he was doing what he had to do to keep his family going.

Their oldest child, son Elijah, always loved to cook. By the age of eight, he had even developed his own salad dressing recipe. He loved to put it together when they were visiting with friends or relatives. Whenever he would prepare it, everyone's reaction was always the same: they would tell him he needed to go into business and sell it.

By the time he was 10 years old, he persisted that he wanted to sell his dressing. He convinced Brenda to check with the local commercial kitchen to see if it was a viable product to take to market. With the understanding the idea of launching a salad dressing business would be a great learning experience for Elijah, Brenda set up a meeting with the man who ran the kitchen. Initially, she was pleasantly surprised he entertained the idea of meeting with a 10-year-old.

For their first meeting, he had asked Elijah and Brenda to bring a sample of their dressing and the recipe. As the man reviewed the recipe, he noted it contained honey. He mentioned Moloka'i at one point had been the largest exporter of kiawe honey, a highly desirable honey from the blooms of the mesquite hardwood kiawe trees. He noted if they could bring back production of kiawe honey to Moloka'i, they would really have a winner.

Brenda politely thanked him, but she declined. The family didn't have any experience with bees, and she didn't want to start. Their focus was still to see the viability of Elijah's salad dressing.

The next time Brenda and Elijah spoke to the man at the commercial kitchen, he mentioned the fact the U.S. Department of Agriculture was offering an agricultural grant for products grown on Moloka'i. The grant could potentially be for $100,000. He encouraged Brenda to apply.

Brenda and Denny spoke and decided it might be worth a try. They checked with the grant administrator. He actually wasn't sure honey production would qualify, so they asked him to check. After confirming bees were viewed as livestock, and in fact would be eligible, Brenda and Denny officially put in for a grant.

During the application review process, they immersed themselves into learning everything they could about beekeeping. They spoke to every beekeeper they could find and were able to gain a lot of knowledge through them. They even found an O'ahu-based beekeeper who had some hives on Moloka'i. He was very forthcoming with what he knew, and when he came to Moloka'i, he even showed them how to process the honey.

They also learned the history of kiawe honey. After the beekeepers of the 1920s and '30s closed down, a man resurrected it many years later. Tired of the changes in weather patterns, he eventually decided to close down his business, leaving the Moloka'i honey business just a memory for several decades. The Kaneshiros were able to speak to him and also gain further insight about kiawe honey. It was during this time in which they also found a beekeeper on another island to provide them with 25 hives of bees, which would be enough to get them started.

When they moved to the interview process of the grant, the Kaneshiros engaged the entire family. Everybody in the family would have a role in the business, and they all participated in their interview/presentation.

After the process was complete, they received a $25,000 grant. This was less than they applied for but was enough to secure equipment and get them started in the business.

They called the only beekeeper who had been willing to sell them any hives and said they were ready for their 25 hives. Unfortunately, the beekeeper told them the situation had changed, and he was no longer willing to sell them the bees he had promised.

The Kaneshiros were devastated. They had been trying to find bee hives out in the wild with no luck. There was no other beekeeper willing to sell them bees. While they didn't want to disappoint everyone who had worked to help them in securing the grant, it appeared they were out of options. In a desperate attempt, the family designed posters which said, "Bee Removal Service – 50% Off." They thought if they could get a few calls, maybe they could start slowly and build their business up over time.

Unbelievably, the phone started ringing… and ringing… and ringing. Each call meant several things for the Kaneshiros:

1). Hives were secured to get their business off the ground.

2). They began getting an immediate income, something they hadn't anticipated until much later in the season after the honey was produced.

3). With each call they left with not only a customer but a friend. They had come to Moloka'i feeling like outsiders. Soon they were embraced by the community and were building customers and interest in their honey with each bee removal.

Once they got their bees, Brenda, Denny and family were in the honey business. Initially, they were as low tech as can be. They used an extractor which they had to hand-crank to spin the honey out of the combs. They found jars shaped like bees, though being just clear glass it didn't have the features detailed. Brenda filled them in with permanent marker. Whether it was simply a pent-up demand for kiawe honey, clever marketing with the bee bottles or simply the charm of the Kaneshiros, the product immediately began selling for them.

Kiawe honey is very unique. The early yield from the blooms is a clear honey that almost looks like Karo™ syrup. Later, the pollination yields a honey which is golden yellow in color. Both are delicious, but the signature and most coveted honey is the early-bloom clear version.

Unlike most varietals of honey, kiawe has a very short opportunity when it can be harvested. Once the bees cap it in the honeycomb, you only have about three weeks to remove it before it is crystallized.

As the Kaneshiros were still learning the ins and outs of managing the honey production of their bees, they attempted a vacation during the middle of honey season. They thought they had everything securely calculated, but when they returned, they were saddened to learn their honey was already crystallized. They missed the 3-week window to get the fresh honey.

Figuring it was loaded with nutrients, they began simply discarding the crystallized honey in their garden. Just as they had when they struggled with what to do when they couldn't find bees, the Kaneshiros turned to their faith for answers during these troubling times. Facing the loss of an entire season, they wanted to know what to do. Through prayer, the answer did come to them. They decided to try to carve up the crystallized honey to serve it as honeycomb. This would end up being a favorite of the local restaurants and is something they have continued to offer every season since.

Once again, keeping faith over all else had worked well for the Kaneshiros. This truly was put to the test when a large retailer came calling, looking to sell their honey.

One of the stipulations was the retailer wanted their own label on the product. The Kaneshiros were okay with the idea as long as it acknowledged it was from Moloka'i and it had their motto on it (To God BEE the glory). When the retailer produced their sample label, it was missing the motto. Brenda and Denny informed the retailer that despite the fact they were offered the largest order they ever received, without the phrase on the bottle, they wouldn't sell it. The retailer refused to add the motto, and the Kaneshiros went with their faith, and their heart, and elected to refuse the order. Just like every year before or since, by the end of the year, they had sold all of their inventory.

Even though they got sidetracked making the honey, eventually they got back around to working on getting their son's salad dressing to market. It also sold well. Too good, if that is possible. Soon their son had offers from a steakhouse in Washington and a company in Canada looking to buy it. He was ready to quit school and sell it full-time. His parents had to ease him back a little to keep him focused on his schooling and only offer it locally. It was a great experience for him, and all three of Brenda and Denny's daughters who have followed suit and brought their own products to market as well.

The family continues to explore more opportunities for their brand. For a while they were exporting their product to Japan after it appeared in a Japanese travel magazine thanks to their old friend the beekeeper who had a few hives on Moloka'i and helped teach them the business. His wife sells some of their honey at a farmers' market on O'ahu, and she helped get it featured in the magazine, creating a demand for it in Japan. They are currently in negotiations with new exporters and hope to begin offering it there again soon.

Soon after they launched the business, Denny was able to give up the odd jobs he was doing to support the family. Everyone helps out with the family business… though it has gotten a little harder recently. Their son has graduated high school, and after some missionary work, he has settled in O'ahu where he is pursuing a commercial pilot's license.

There also have been a few hiccups along the way…
- A few years ago there was a forest fire which took many of the family's hives.

- Recently, they've been struggling with a beetle which infests the hives (they place natural traps with oil that the beetles fall into and can't get out of as chemicals are never used in their processing).

- They lost their "certified organic" designation when the local company which certified organizations on Moloka'i stopped offering certifications. They couldn't afford to bring someone from the Mainland to provide their certification so they kept the processes of certified organic companies, but lost the "official designation."

Despite the issues they have faced over the years, the Kaneshiros wouldn't change a thing. Through hard work, the strength of their family and a commitment to their faith, they've succeeded at every step of the way in making Moloka'i Meli the best product it can be for their customers.

The Kaneshiros in their beekeeping gear in front of some of the apiary

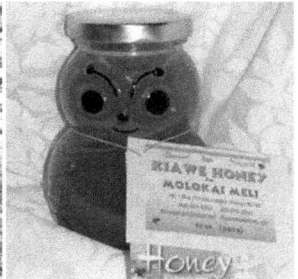

The Firsts: Elijah's salad dressing which started it all, the first wild hive they collected and the original bee jars Brenda used to color the features in with permanent black marker

A kiawe blossom

Collection of wild bees remains a key part of the Kaneshiros business

The most important job: gathering the honey

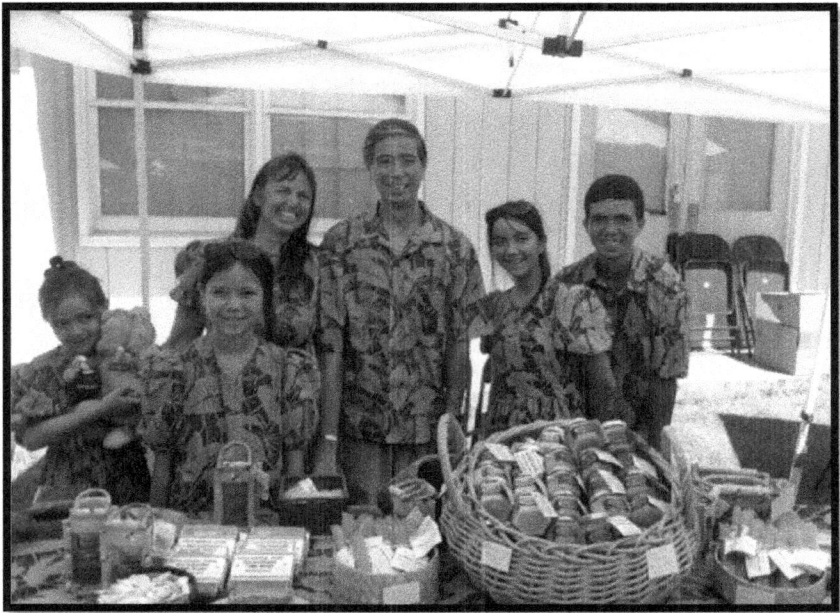
The Kaneshiro family showing off their product lineup

Chapter 14: Hot Sauce
Adoboloco

Kīhei, Maui, HI
(808) 874 - 1876

adoboloco.com
bacak@adoboloco.com

Established
2011

Leadership
Tim Parsons, Owner

Products
Organic hot sauces in a variety of heat and flavor profiles

Don't you wish Cypress Hill's song _Insane in the Membrane_ started with these lines, "Who you trying to get crazy with, ése? Don't you know I'm Adoboloco?"...

Growing up in Kīhei on Maui, Tim Parsons focused on one thing for a career: he wanted to be an artist. In school, he excelled in art classes and photography. By his junior year, he had developed an impressive portfolio which he planned to use to get a scholarship to help him get the schooling he would need to fulfill his dream.

The more people (inside and outside of the art world) he spoke to about life as an artist, the more he became concerned. Basic essentials, like, well, you know, eating or a place to live might be difficult as a true artist - "True artist" being someone who's income is solely dependent on creating and selling their own original artwork.

He had a backup plan, though.

He decided to become a graphic artist. As such, he would be paid for his art and creativity, and it would be a little more structured and a reliable source of income.

He studied graphic design in Honolulu. When his schooling was complete, he decided to look outside of Hawai'i for work. Not because of lack of opportunity there, but due to the fact he had met a woman named Summer while she was vacationing on Maui. This chance encounter would begin a relationship, and the two would fall in love and get married. Tim sought work in her home state of Oregon.

With his artistic and graphic design skills, he was able to find work as a sign painter and printer. Then he became an art director in an ad agency. There he designed websites. This was a time when the dotcom boom was taking off so there was a lot of opportunity, and Tim was good at the work. The company was winning all kinds of awards and accolades for the designs they were putting together.

When the dotcom bubble burst, and all of the work began to dry up, Tim lost his job. He was left in shock and vowed to never work for someone else again. He began collecting his unemployment as he started to look into the idea of starting his own business.

Running his own business would offer him freedom, and he liked the idea of being able to control his own destiny without a chance of being blindsided and out of a job again. Plus, it seemed to be in his blood. He had three siblings, and they each had their own successful businesses they had started.

As he began to get ideas together for a new business, the Unemployment Office called him and requested a meeting. He wondered if he was in some sort of trouble for seeking to start his own company rather than trying to set up interviews to work for someone else.

How could they know, though?

Tim was taken totally off-guard when the team at the Unemployment Office told him they had reviewed his file. With his talents, they were willing to pay his full unemployment benefits if he was willing to open up a new business. There was a need for a graphic design/website builder in the market so it made sense to continue to pay him as he built a business. The only stipulation was he had to have meetings and run a business plan through a professor at Oregon State University.

Wow!

Not only were they willing to give Tim financial support through a very difficult time, he was now getting professional assistance to do so. It really could not have gone any better.

Tim was able to quickly get back on his feet with his business. Many of his clients were in the tech-friendly area of the San Francisco Bay. With the bulk of his customer base already away from his home base of Oregon, he realized he wasn't tied to the area. Tim was ready to get back home to Maui, and Summer was willing to get out of the cold as well and build a new life/raise a family on Maui.

In 2010, they moved back to Tim's hometown of Kīhei. It was great to be home near his mother and siblings. They also made a big lifestyle change with the move to Hawai'i as they elected to homeschool their children.

One of their first homeschooling initiatives was to create a project where the kids could work together and learn from the project and each other. The family came up with the idea of a garden with each person (including Tim and Summer) growing an item in the garden. One of kids decided to go with jalapeno peppers, so they planted approximately 100 plants.

When all of the plants began thriving, the Parsons were rewarded with a bounty of jalapenos. So many, they couldn't possibly consume all of them. They decided to start making their own sauce and share it with friends and family.

Everyone whom they shared it with wanted to buy a bottle so Tim started to look into what it would take to run a hot sauce business. It took a year of licensing, inspections, insurance and packaging to get a company off the ground, but in 2011, the Parsons family launched Adoboloco, their own hot sauce brand.

Tim began calling on stores to carry Adoboloco. He had one of his first calls result in a manager requesting 2 cases based on the story of the local family farm producing it. From there, more distribution was easy. Simply talking about other stores it was in and letting them sample the product while telling the story of a family creating the sauce using all organic growing principles made distribution almost as much fun as producing it.

By 2012, Adoboloco had grown to the point where Tim was able to shutdown his graphic arts business and focus solely on the hot sauce company with the family. For him, it's a joy everyday to be able to work in a business side-by-side with the people he loves most in the world.

Each family member has a key role to make Adoboloco successful.

Tim is in charge of making the hot sauce, marketing, website design, sales and customer service.

Summer handles all of the internet shipping orders.

Oldest son Xander is responsible for labeling and inventory management.

The Parsons' younger son Harrison handles loading and unloading of freight.

Daughter Scarlet is the designated chili pepper picker, a task she manages first thing every morning.

As a family business, everyone pitches in and helps one another. They also help out with any other jobs which pop up as well as tending to the plants. Of course, running the farm goes beyond just peppers. They have chickens, pigs and goats for livestock. They also grow avocados, taro, papaya, citrus, vegetables and bananas.

Tim sees a future of continued growth for Adoboloco. He has built the brand with a combination of social media and grass roots marketing. They are very involved in the local community, appearing at farmers' markets. They even began their own campaign of "Free Bottle Day" where they give out full-sized bottles to stunned attendees as a means to build brand awareness.

The ultimate goal for Tim would be to continue to build the brand up as they have been doing and at some point turn the business over to his children to run. It seems with a story which encompasses much more than hot sauce they should continue to build on what they have. Their story of family, organic gardening and promoting Hawaiian agriculture is one many would love to hear.

Of course, while the story may get their interest, the sauce keeps bringing them back. It really wants to make you say:

Who you trying to get crazy with, ése?

Don't you know I'm Adoboloco?

Adoboloco Photo Album

Tim Parsons

The entire Parsons family has a role in Adoboloco

Bhut Jalokia, a.k.a. the Ghost Pepper, is one of the varietals which can be found in an Adoboloco sauce

Hot sauce production

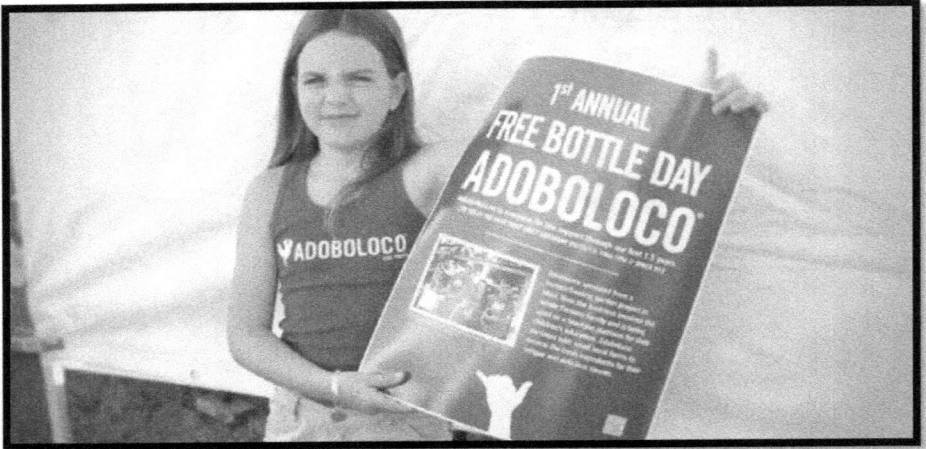

An annual "Free Bottle Day" is one of the promotions
Adoboloco uses

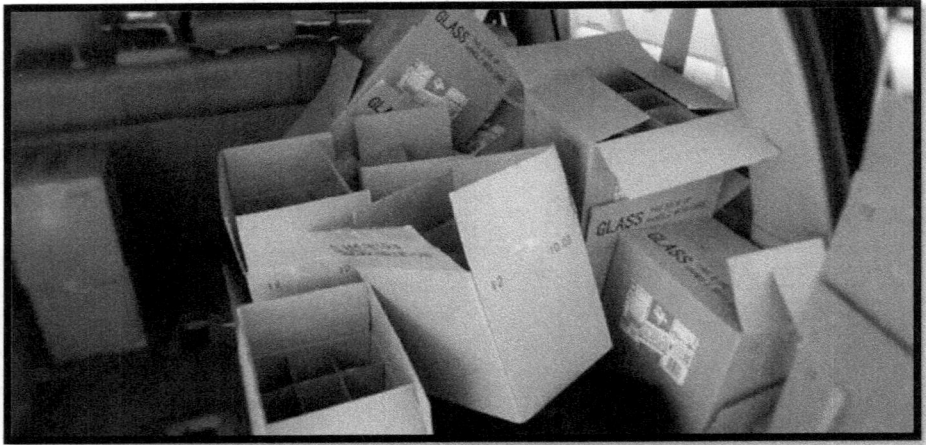

Free Bottle Day – The aftermath

Detail of the packaging/label

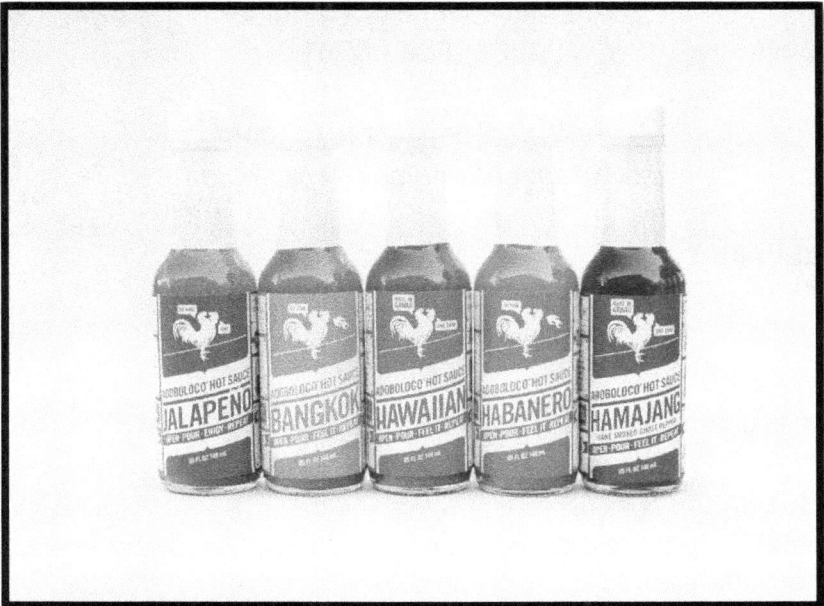

Adoboloco product line-up

Chapter 15: Ice Cream
Tropical Dreams Ice Cream

66-1250 Lalamilo Farm Road
Kamuela, Hawai'i, HI 96734
(888) 888 - 8031

tropicaldreamsicecream.com
info@tropicaldreamsicecream.com

Established
1983

Leadership
John and Nancy Edney, Owners

Products
Tropical Dreams super-premium ice cream, Big Island and Hilo Homemade premium ice creams, real Italian-style gelato, sorbets, frozen yogurts, sherbets, and Hula Cow Fresh Big Island Butter

Decision time: #1: Porta-Potty Business or #2: Super Premium Ice Cream Company…

John Edney can make a tough decision. No one would question that.

His best decision was an easy one, though.

During the course of a 30-year career in the transportation industry, John had plenty of opportunities to make judgment calls on many challenging issues. Much of his working life was spent at a school bus company which ran 6,000 buses in the western United States. His senior vice president role gave him responsibilities in sales, marketing and human resources.

His job had taken he and his wife Nancy from their home state of California to Texas and, ultimately, to Poughkeepsie, New York. The Texas move had come via a transfer under the ownership of the bus company. His move to Poughkeepsie came after an acquisition of his corporation. It had been bought out by a multi-national organization which specialized in privatizing public entities like railroads and airports.

The corporation's entrée into the U.S. market had been with the bus company, and then their first privatization project was the airport in Poughkeepsie. John was put in charge of running the airport while they searched for a permanent director for the facility.

Nancy was a pastry chef. Her culinary experience included working pastry for noted celebrity chef Wolfgang Puck.

Nancy and John had always loved Hawai'i. In fact, they were married on the Big Island. In 1998 they bought some land where they would eventually build a home.

After John finished his work at the airport, he and Nancy were ready to make the move to Hawai'i full-time. Not ready for retirement, they began searching for opportunities.

John actually laughs pretty heartily when he reflects on some of the businesses at which he was looking. His favorite to mention was a porta-potty business in addition to Tropical Dreams Ice Cream.

It really wasn't much of a decision.

Tropical Dreams had a great reputation, an excellent product, and it appeared it would benefit from both John's business acumen and Nancy's background in the culinary world. Tropical Dreams Ice Cream would also help them fulfill their own tropical dream of a life in Hawai'i.

They were set to close the deal on September 12, 2001. When the events of September 11 did end up delaying the closing and the troubling issues of the day led them to some self-reflection about the purchase. Ultimately, they did move forward with the purchase and closed the deal a few days later on September 18, 2001.

What was to become Tropical Dreams Ice Cream began in 1983 as a company making macadamia nut butter. By 1987 they had expanded the product line to ice cream, which is what they soon would be focusing on solely.

At 18% butterfat, Tropical Dreams is an ultra-creamy product with low overrun (little air), making it very dense. It is officially categorized as a super premium ice cream (compare it to national brands which would typically have a butterfat content in the 10% range).

One of the factors which contributes to the quality of the product is the fact the company produces its ice cream in 20 or 40 quart batch freezers. This small batch approach mirrors, on a larger scale, the process which most consumers who make ice cream at home are familiar. Conversely, most larger manufacturers of ice cream utilize a continuous production format which yields much quicker production but tends to sacrifice flavor.

When John and Nancy purchased the company, the owner had been focusing primarily on the hotel, restaurant and ice cream shop trade. They wanted to expand their wholesale packaged product production.

Once their packaging was ready, John began actively selling the product himself. As the word got out, he was fielding as many calls to carry his product as he was making himself.

John and Nancy also brought a strategy of growth through acquisition and licensing. In 2003 they made their first strategic growth purchase of Hilo Homemade, another ice cream company based on the Big Island of Hawai'i. Hilo Homemade was another premium product (16% butter fat) and was run as an independent label as it had before the purchase of the company.

Knowing the challenges of expanding to the Mainland would be difficult, John and Nancy elected to go the route of licensing agreement when they established partners looking to bring their product to new markets. They added distribution in both Southern California and Salt Lake City through licensing agreements, which allowed partners to produce ice cream, using their recipes in defined territories.

Their most unique licensing agreement came from a very unusual situation. One of the customers for their Hilo Homemade ice cream was a Japanese-national who ran a dipping shop on the Big Island. He had maintained a strong Japanese clientele base by advertising the brand in Japan in tourist publications. This resulted in many individuals from the large tourism trade to Hawai'i from Japan visiting his shop on the Big Island.

He moved back home to Japan for a time but had difficulty with his visa when he tried to come back to Hawai'i. Rather than getting involved in a prolonged fight over his visa situation, he contacted John and Nancy to establish a licensing agreement, allowing him to bring the product to his hometown of Kugenuma, Japan. Through many years of advertising, it was an incredibly positive situation for him to be able to sell to a customer base he had built in his hometown.

The company's latest acquisition occurred in 2010 when they purchased another local 16% butterfat ice cream called Big Island. Like both Tropical Dreams and Hilo Homemade, the company had a stellar reputation. The owner had always been committed to only the finest ingredients.

A perfect example of their dedication to their product was their strawberry cheesecake flavor. The owners would fly in strawberry cheesecake directly from Brooklyn, New York to ensure they were offering the best product possible. For John and Nancy, their idea to run this brand was simple – keep doing what the previous owners had done and use their established distribution channels to grow business.

The company, as a whole, has also been recognized for its quality commitments. Tropical Dreams Ice Cream is the only ice cream company to be recognized by the State Department of Agriculture for Hawai'i with its Seal of Quality. This prestigious designation recognizes the company for sourcing more than 50% of its ingredients locally.

With the Big Island, Maui and O'ahu saturated with their product, they've begun looking elsewhere for growth. The idea of shipping to a warehouse in southern California seems like a viable way to grow their business in the western portion of the United States. John's son lives in Los Angeles so he can actually help out by working with the company's partners as they make this move.

Making this project successful will involve securing the company's own warehouse in southern California. John has made the choice to go all-in on this approach to take Tropical

Dreams Ice Cream to the next level and is actively involved in this new business approach for the organization.

It seems to be the perfect move. After all, John's usually pretty good with his decisions.

Tropical Dreams Ice Cream Photo Album

Nancy and John Edney

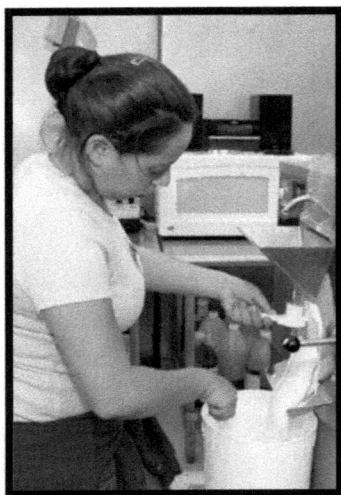

Making ice cream

Packing ice cream

Delivering product

Tropical Dreams has great marketing shots of its products...
depicted here is their coconut ice cream

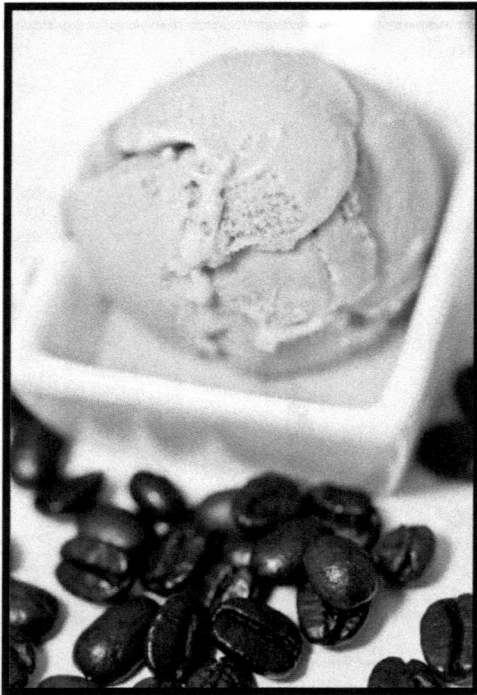

Tropical Dreams' Kona coffee ice cream

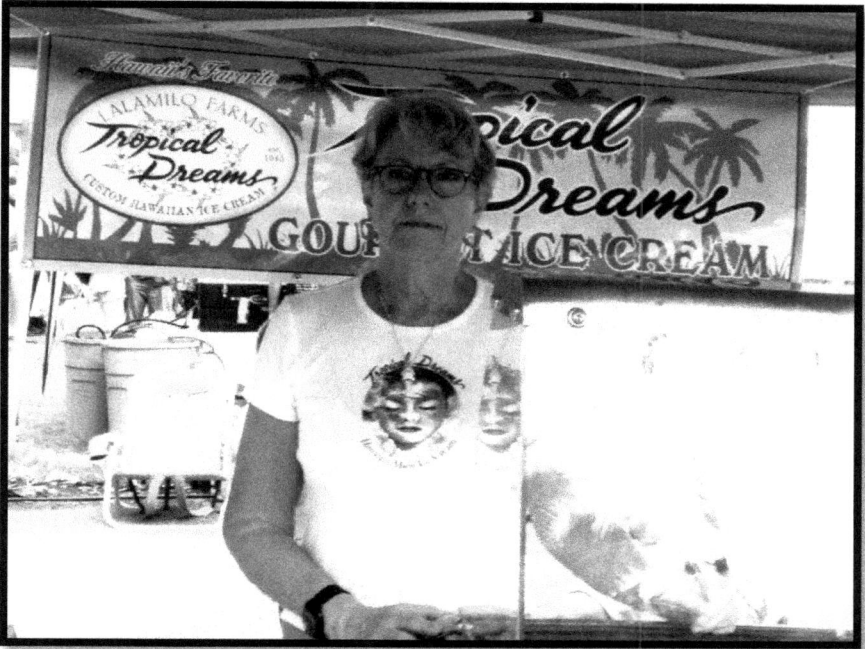
Nancy out in the community representing the brand

Tropical Dreams product lineup

Chapter 16: Ice Pops
Shaka Pops

P.O. Box 532673
Kīhei, Maui, HI 96753
(808) 442 - 2926

info@shakapopsmaui.com
shakapopsmaui.com

Established
2012

Leadership
Christine Vestfals & Larry Lutz, Owners

Products
Rotating flavors of island ice pops in both dairy and non-dairy versions

(Note: Popsicle™ is a registered trademark of Unilever®)

The ice pop is the new cupcake...

Christine Vestfals and Larry Lutz have hit the entrepreneurial version of a Powerball™ jackpot. They are married and living in Hawai'i (not a bad start). Tired of the corporate life, they have managed to start a business there meaning they get to work together sharing the joy of building their business from scratch (it's getting better). Building any business has a certain level of stress, but how can you not have a smile on your face going to work each day when your product is ice pops?

Jackpot!

Considering Christine grew up in Toronto, and Larry in Kansas, it didn't seem likely this story would be told. Love found a way to bring these two together, though.

Growing up, Christine's mother was ahead of her time. She was already on the health conscious bandwagon, cutting out sugar, sweets and processed foods. Occasionally, she would make ice pops from fresh fruit as a treat for the family. This didn't play heavily into Christine's idea of starting her company, but she would draw upon this experience later in life when she and Larry would start Shaka Pops. As an adult, Christine wanted to move away from the brutally cold winters of Toronto, so she moved to the Canadian equivalent of Florida: Vancouver. (Actually, Vancouver is south of Toronto and features a beautiful Pacific Northwest landscape and much milder temperatures. As you read through this chapter you will notice Christine moving a little farther south with each relocation.)

Larry grew up in Holton, Kansas, and after graduation from the University of Kansas, he lived and worked for a short time for the Smithsonian Institute® on an island in the Panama Canal. When he completed his time there, he worked for a brief time in Kansas before joining a friend who had moved to Seattle and encouraged him to move there as well. Since he was looking for a change, he decided to take the plunge, and moved to Washington.

In 2000, on a guys' weekend to Vancouver, Larry happened to meet Christine enjoying a girls' night out. The two fell in love and carried out a long-distance romance with Larry making the trip back-and-forth from Seattle to Vancouver every weekend, something which was made particularly challenging following the events of September 11th.

When they decided to get married, Christine and Larry chose Maui for a destination wedding. It was the first trip for both of them, but they instantly fell in love with the beauty and charm of Maui. They visited again on their first anniversary and continued to vacation there as often as they could.

After living in Seattle for a while, they moved to California in the San Francisco Bay area where Christine worked in the wine industry, and Larry went back to school to work on his MBA while continuing to work full-time at an auto dealership.

During one of their vacations in Maui, they ran into a couple who were also married there at the same time they were. They were surprised to find out they had had decided to move and now were full-time residents of Maui. When Christine expressed an interest to move there as well, the couple encouraged them to join them in Hawai'i. They even spoke about potential business ideas of a wine bar or cupcake shop, two things which were in surprisingly short supply. While Larry and Christine thought it was the ultimate dream to move to Maui, they seemed pretty entrenched in their lives in California.

When Christine unexpectedly lost her job, she thought she would get right back on her feet with another corporate job. With a solid resume and impressive work history, she soon had interviews lined up and quickly got a job offer. As she contemplated the job, she kept thinking how another job like the one she just had could end exactly how her previous job did. Where would she be then?

She decided to turn down the offer and talk to Larry about making the move to Maui full-time and starting a business there. He was supportive of looking into it, so she began researching the merits of a wine bar (it was the winner over the cupcake shop since Christine wasn't a baker).

It seemed like the wine bar was going to be expensive and filled with regulations, so she started leaning towards cupcakes. Then she read an article about how "ice pops were the new cupcakes." The article implied cupcakes were played out, and ice pops were the next trendy food item lending a new palette for the creative chefs looking for a delicious dessert to experiment with.

Thinking back to her days as a youth in Toronto where her mother made ice pops as a snack, Christine instantly thought it was the right business for her. With a clear direction now set, Christine and Larry focused on starting an ice pops business in Maui. Larry even wrote the business plan as a paper for his final project to complete his MBA.

Three months later, Christine headed to Maui, and Larry stayed behind to get their affairs in order in California. She began working on the ice pops, drawing upon a lifetime of cooking and instincts to come up with her recipes. Of course, hers were going to be vastly different from the ones her mother prepared for the family when Christine was a girl growing up in Toronto. Like Mom's, they were going to be made with fresh fruit, but she wasn't going to prepare them in an ice cream machine. The machines are commonly used by ice pop companies, but introduce whipped air into the pops. While Christine would miss out on the benefits of stretching ingredients by adding air with an ice cream machine, the end result for her pops would be an intensely flavorful treat, which was solid and dense.

The goal was for Larry to continue to work full-time in California until he sold their home and then he would work in Maui while Christine built up the ice pops business. Once they got the business large enough to support the two of them, they would then work side-by-side at Shaka Pops, the name they came up with for their new business.

Their plans were turned upside down when Larry's employer found out about his plans to quit once he sold his home so they decided to let him go immediately. After an unsuccessful search on Hawai'i to find a job matching his work experience and education, they decided to forgo the idea of having Larry work another job and instead immediately start working together on building their business.

Their product was very different than the sugar water most people in the U.S. think of when it comes to ice pops. Their product was more along the lines of the popular Mexican dessert known as paletas. These popular ice pop-style treats are denser than the U.S. version. Shaka Pops feature recipes made with real fruit and are only flavored with cane sugar, honey or the natural fruit. Their pops can be found in non-dairy (fruit/fruit juice only) and dairy/fruit/fruit juice versions. With the abundance and variety of local fruits, Shaka Pops have a seemingly unlimited potential for new ideas and combinations.

Christine and Larry started out with a custom ice cream tricycle they would bring to events and farmers' markets. The face-to-face interaction between Christine and Larry and their potential customers was just what they needed to educate individuals about their unique treats. It wasn't uncommon for someone to wonder who would pay $4 for an ice pop, then give them a try after speaking to Christine and Larry. Afterwards, Christine and Larry would be amazed to see the customer who had moments before been questioning who would buy a $4 pop then trying to convince others to join them in enjoying a Shaka Pop.

Not being from Hawai'i, Christine and Larry were concerned how the locals would take to them and their business. They have been amazed how individuals have not only embraced their product but have offered their help every step of the way. As they began to look at getting into stores, it wasn't uncommon for individuals they met selling ice pops at farmers' markets to encourage them and offer ideas about contacts they had to assist them into getting into local stores.

Christine is continuously experimenting and adding new flavors. Their most popular flavor is Lava Flow which is a piña colada and strawberry flavored pop.

Not every flavor can be a winner, though. Christine cites a peach pop as her least popular flavor to date. The small, locally-sourced peaches were so tart she had to keep adding honey (she only uses natural ingredients) to sweeten the pops. By the time she was finished, there was no taste of peach, only honey. Not necessarily a bad taste, just not something you can market as a "peach pop."

Christine lists her Mayan Chocolate pop as a potential star in the making. They offer it around Cinco de Mayo and for special events. It hasn't caught on just yet, as the dairy pop featuring cinnamon and cayenne scares many off before they try it. Those, who do give it a taste, tend to like it. Over time, she thinks it will continue to build a following.

For Larry and Christine, the possibilities of their company still seem limitless. They use two carts to sell their pops (one stationed in the same place five days a week and the other which moves to events and markets), and they have a large presence in stores on Maui. They are in the process of expanding distribution to the rest of the Islands of Hawai'i. Long term they see increased distribution which will likely include the U.S. Mainland.

For now, they are happy with their entrepreneurial Powerball™ jackpot and a company which affords them the luxury of being able to give back to the community. It appears the future for Christine and Larry is exceptionally bright with Shaka Pops. Unless, of course, Christine decides she wants to open Dingo Pops in Sydney, Australia. It makes sense she would end up there because we know one thing for sure, if she decides to move, she's heading south!

Shaka Pops Photo Album

Larry Lutz & Christine Vestfals

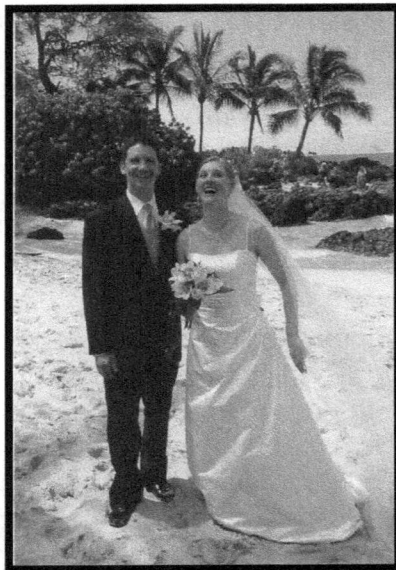

Larry and Christine on a Maui beach on their wedding day

Christine and Larry at Whale Day in February of 2012, their very first day in business (with friends Leah Young and Chris Kanyo who were married in Maui at the same time as Christine and Larry)

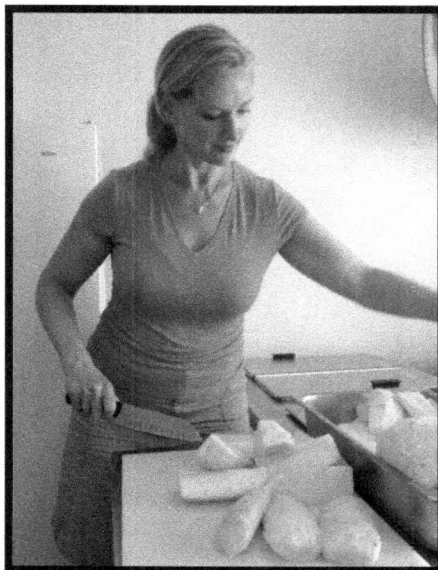

Christine in the kitchen preparing to make some pops

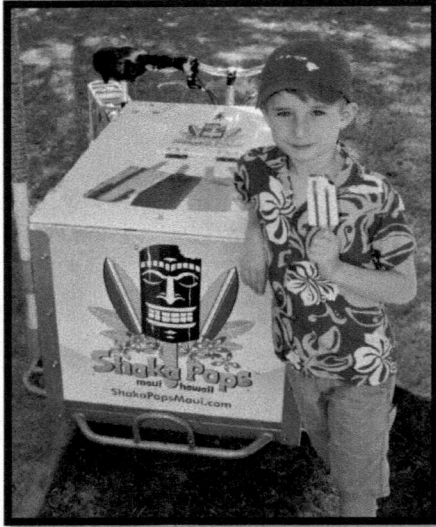

You can get Shaka Pops at an event…

…or in a store

Pop detail: Tangerine Cream

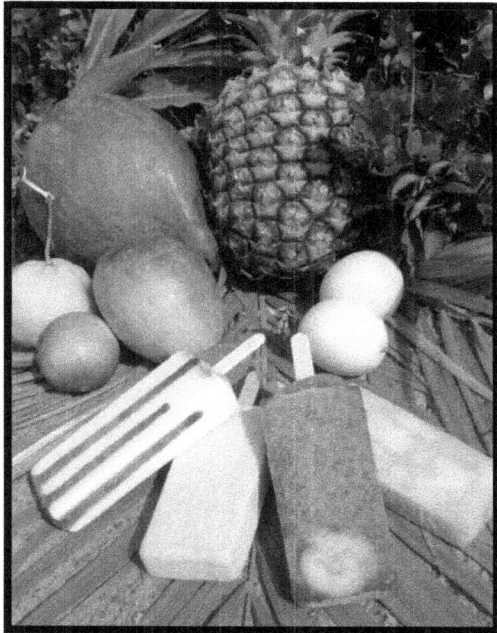

Shaka Pops product lineup

Chapter 17: Kona Coffee
Hula Daddy Kona Coffee

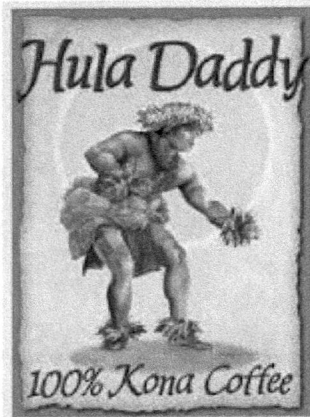

74-4944 Mamalahoa Highway
Holualoa, HI 96725
(808) 327 - 9744

huladaddy.com
huladaddy@huladaddy.com

Established
2002

Leadership
Karen and Lee Paterson, Owners

Products
Kona coffee

Wanna talk fresh coffee? How about a place where you can buy your coffee while it's still warm from the roaster...

Karen and Lee Paterson met in a professional organization both were involved with in their hometown of Los Angeles. Karen was in human resources, and Lee was a litigation attorney. Karen served on the board for the professional organization, and Lee served as General Counsel. They fell in love and got married.

Seemingly, these young, urban professionals had the perfect life: great jobs and living in an exciting city. They had a different idea of the perfect life, though. They had enjoyed vacationing in Hawai'i and began to think about how they could make a move to make it their full-time residence.

Their plan was something in the agriculture industry. They basically got the choices down to two: macadamia nuts or Kona coffee. In the end, they made the choice to go the coffee route.

It was something they had a common interest in, and they believed there was a built-in audience to "buy American" when it came to coffee while macadamia nuts seemed to be much more commoditized. As they reflect back years later, they would end up being happy with this decision as more macadamia nuts are being harvested from other countries. Their concerns appeared to be spot-on. At the same time, the demand for coffee grown in Hawai'i continues to rise.

They brought a passion to their business but not a whole lot of experience. Lee's grandparents had a farm when he was a child, but that was the extent of their combined agricultural knowledge. They dipped their toes in the water by growing some coffee trees at their California home. Living on the coast, away from the occasional freezing temperatures inland, they were able to successfully grow coffee. Admittedly, the coffee wasn't great, but they felt comfortable moving forward with their plans.

The easiest route to entering the coffee business would have been to buy an existing farm. That would have likely not only been much more expensive, but also they would have been buying someone else's coffee. Karen and Lee wanted the coffee they would offer to be uniquely their own.

They were pleased to find an 11-acre parcel of pastureland available in the town of Holualoa, right in the heart of the Kona coffee district. They purchased the farm, moved from Los Angeles, and went to work.

The first step was to gain some knowledge about the industry. They met with an established coffee manager who gave them insight on the proper planting of the farm.

The next step was to completely bulldoze the property and then begin planting. With their 11 acres, they had room for 7,000 trees. Coffee trees take five years of growing before they bear fruit. The Patersons sped up the process a bit by planting two year-old-saplings. Even so, they still had 3 years of farming with no income.

It was during this time they became fully immersed in the industry. Through organizations like the Kona Coffee Council, Kona Farmers Association, and The Hawaiian Coffee Association, they found the shared knowledge of individuals already in the business to be invaluable. Individuals in these organizations welcomed them and were more than willing to share their experiences and best practices for success.

Coffee trees can grow up to 40' in height. The Patersons pruned their trees to a maximum of 10 – 14'. This makes it much easier to harvest the fruit.

The coffee beans come from the fruit on the trees which looks like cherries. The fruit itself is sweet and doesn't taste at all like coffee. Like the pit of a cherry, the coffee bean sits inside of the fruit.

The fruit ripens from January – July (going from green to yellow to red). The individual blossoms ripen at different times so there must be weekly harvests during the season. The pickers carry around sticks with ropes. The sticks are tossed over the branches and then the ropes are pulled down bringing the branch to a height where the fruit can be picked. They stand on the rope while they collect the ripened fruit. They then simply step off and go on to the next branch. An experienced picker can collect about 150 – 200 lbs. of fruit a day.

The ripened fruit is then put onto a sorting table. The process Karen and Lee established was to only use the best beans from their harvest. Any under or overripe fruit is removed. This will be sold to other producers who aren't as picky about the quality of their product.

The next quality control step for the company is to float the beans in water. Any beans that float will not meet the quality standards of Hula Daddy Kona Coffee and will be sold to other coffee producers.

The beans are fermented in water for 36 hours and then are put in a pulper to remove the fruit. The next step is to place them on covered drying racks. The greenhouse effect of the covered racks causes the temperature to rise to about 120 degrees.

The beans are then milled to remove the skin (kind of like skin on a shelled peanut). Once this has been completed, the beans are ready to roast. Roasting the coffee takes about 12 – 14 minutes, and when finished, it is ready to be bagged and sold (or to drink).

Hula Daddy has an onsite Visitors Center where guests can try all of the varieties of coffee the company offers. They even make a caffeinated tea out of the fruit from the coffee trees. Like the fruit itself, the tea doesn't taste like coffee.

At the Visitors Center guests enjoy great views of Kona and the harbor. They also go on tours of the plantation where they can see the coffee trees growing and even taste the fruit. A favorite activity, especially for kids during the tours, is to see if guests can spot the free-roaming chameleons they have on the farm. The chameleons do not damage the trees and eat bugs so they are welcome guests. Their natural color-changing ability makes it tough to spot them, but kids seem to enjoy seeking them out.

The tours end back at Hula Daddy's store where the coffee is being roasted. If they like, they can buy the coffee they witness being roasted right as it comes out of the roaster. Obviously, there isn't a way to buy fresher coffee than that!

A great visitor's experience will sell coffee, but a superior product will keep those customers coming back, and it is exactly what Hula Daddy has been able to deliver. They have won multiple awards for their coffee (including Coffee Farm of the Year by *Hawai'i Magazine*® in 2013).

They have their coffees rated by Coffee Review® out of Berkley, California. This independent third-party organization serves as a barometer for the industry, rating coffees on a 100 point scale. The highest score ever bestowed by the organization is a 97. Hula Daddy is pleased to be one of the companies to achieve a 97 with their Kona Sweet in 2013.

Hula Daddy doesn't sell any of their coffee wholesale. All is sold through either on-site purchases or via their website. The company has also expanded operations by adding an additional twenty-seven acres in 2008, bringing their grand total to 38 acres. This additional volume has allowed them to try different types of beans and expand the Hula Daddy line.

The Patersons continue to improve their coffee, focusing on quality and new offerings and by trying different coffees from around the globe. If they stumble across something they like, they try growing it on their farm and adding it to their business mix.

Industry accolades aside, for Karen and Lee the most rewarding aspect of running their business is offering a product to customers which they have created. They get to share something which they have grown, harvested and processed which is uniquely their own. The experience of visiting their farm is both fun and educational for visitors, and they have found the enjoyment their guests get to be a very fulfilling experience for them as well.

Not too bad for a lawyer and human resource professional from Los Angeles!

Hula Daddy Kona Coffee Photo Album

Lee and Karen Paterson

The entrance to the farm

Kona coffee trees

Bunches of the fruit

Fruit in various stages of ripeness

Soon this will be coffee

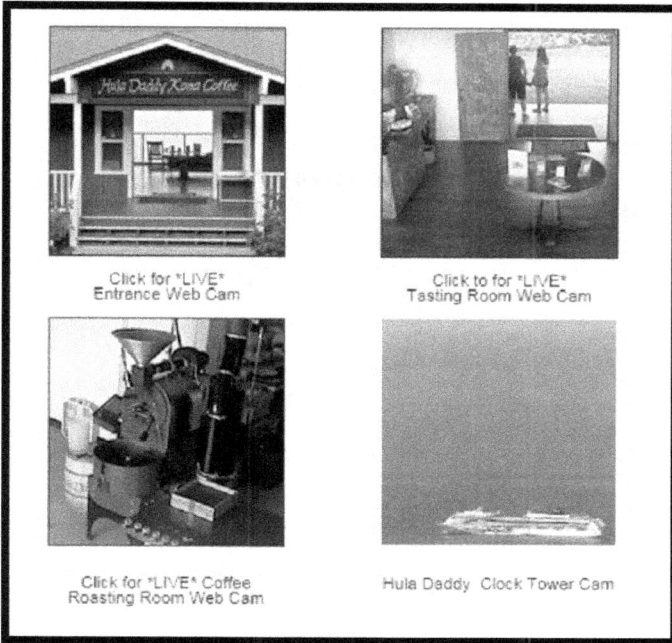

Click for *LIVE*
Entrance Web Cam

Click to for *LIVE*
Tasting Room Web Cam

Click for *LIVE* Coffee
Roasting Room Web Cam

Hula Daddy Clock Tower Cam

Through Hula Daddy's website web cams you can take a virtual tour right from home

Hula Daddy product lineup

Chapter 18: Mushrooms
Hamakua Mushrooms

HAMAKUA MUSHROOMS
Exotically Healthy · Hawaii Fresh

P.O. Box 205
Laupāhoehoe, Hawai'i, HI 96764
(808) 962 - 0017

hamakuamushrooms.com
hamakuafarms@aol.com

Established
2000

Leadership
Robert and Janice Stanga, Owners

Products
Fresh exotic mushrooms

Helicopter Pilot + Interior Designer = Mushrooms?...

Doctors, firefighters, police officers... these are career paths which are often set in childhood. Individuals who gravitate towards these jobs tend to set a plan at a very young age and work their entire life towards their goal of working in these careers.

Mushroom farmers... specifically, Hawaiian mushroom farmers?

Well, that just kinda happens. Take, for instance, the story of Bob and Janice Stanga.

Bob had the first taste of Hawai'i. He was a naval helicopter pilot stationed in Barber's Point, Hawai'i. He loved Hawai'i, and like many others, vowed to come back to live one day. After his discharge he lived in San Diego before settling in Modesto, California, as a pilot/mechanic (after his time in the military he got his commercial pilot's license via the G.I. Bill).

His future wife Janice wasn't a farmer either. She was an interior designer. Entrenched in California, it didn't seem as though life would lead them to an exotic mushroom farm in Hawai'i.

When one of Bob's students mentioned he knew of an opening for a pilot in Hawai'i, he decided to leave California and head back to O'ahu. In Hawai'i, Bob conducted helicopter tours in Waikiki. Later, he purchased his own helicopter and started a utility pilot business in which he would fly crews to the mountains for utility work.

After selling his utility pilot business, Janice and Bob got married and began looking for an opportunity in which they could work together. Looking to take advantage of Hawai'i's 12-months-a-year growing season, Bob was sure he wanted to get into farming. They liked the agriculture of the Big Island so they focused their search there.

After ruling out such standards as lettuce and tomatoes, they were able to narrow themselves down to two possibilities: snails or mushrooms. They were foodies with many friends in the restaurant business. Through both their own evaluations, as well as input from chefs they were friends with, Bob and Janice came to believe the local offerings for both were lesser quality than they had experienced in California.

With no real competition for exotic mushrooms or snails, it appeared both were a viable possibility so they began to research each.

From a 30,000' overview, mushrooms have two types: button and specialty. Button mushrooms are commonly found and not on what the Stangas wanted to focus. They wanted the unique varieties that specialty mushrooms offered. They require a little more work to grow, but yield a meatier, more flavorful mushroom and do not cook down when preparing them. Growing them would involve growing them in a mixture of corn cob, wheat bran and sawdust.

The snails served in restaurants are the California Garden Snail variety so they were readily available. They would need to be brought into Hawai'i which meant working through red tape to bring in live animals. When they began to talk to the State Department of Agriculture, as part of their process to decide mushrooms or snails, the decision was just about made for them.

The State Department of Agriculture, who would later prove to be a great resource for their mushroom business, strongly opposed the concept of a snail farm. There had been an incident with another snail farm on Kaua'i. When the owners of that farm decided they wanted out of the business, they simply threw out the snails. This caused an invasive, non-native species to get introduced, and they didn't want it to happen again.

They followed the advice of the State Department of Agriculture and conducted a feasibility study to see if there was a strong enough market for the product to warrant starting a specialty mushroom business. The study involved them speaking to as many restaurant and store owners as they could to find out if this was something they would be interested in, and if they were, how much they would be willing to pay.

Once it appeared they had adequate demand for their product, Bob and Janice were able to secure a 35 acre plot on the Big Island where they intended to start their farm. Not coming from an agricultural background, they would need to learn the business from the ground up. Their first order of business was to hire a consultant.

The business almost ended before it really got started, though, when the consultant, who had received a significant payment from the Stangas, disappeared. They were left with no way to recover their money and no direction to get their business going.

Their plan was to call other mushroom farmers on the Mainland and share their story. They hoped to find some sympathetic individuals who might be willing to help. Luckily for them, the plan worked. They found a family of successful mushroom farmers who were willing to mentor them on exactly what they needed to do. They headed to California to work side-by-side with these individuals who were simply willing to help because they were good people looking to assist some individuals in need.

It was apparent their luck was taking a turn for the better when they headed back to the Big Island to begin finishing their farm. While building out their growing room, they needed shelving… a lot of it. In fact, they bought out every shelving unit in the style they were using from all seven Costco's® in the State of Hawai'i.

They were taken off-guard when an individual from Costco's® World Headquarters in the state of Washington called them. He wanted to know what they were doing with $14,000 worth of Costco® shelving. When Bob explained his plan to bring locally grown specialty mushrooms to the culinary scene and grocery stores of Hawai'i, he became interested in working with Hamakua to carry its mushrooms in their stores on Hawai'i. Bob hung up the phone with no mushrooms yet, but his first customers already secured!

Bob and Janice have turned visiting Hamakua Mushrooms into a sensory, interactive and learning experience. Individuals can enjoy educational hands-on tours where they stroll the property seeing how Hamakua's mushrooms are grown. They can taste the products on-site as well as being able to shop all varietals. The Stangas often host events like wine and cheese tastings which generate interest in their farm.

Another great addition to the farm has been the Chef's House. This onsite house allows chefs to come and visit the farm with their families. While there, they can prepare dishes, utilizing Hamakua's products in the Chef's House professional kitchen. These are recipes which they then can serve in their own restaurants. This has proven to be a great way to connect with chefs and expand their visibility into restaurants on both the Hawaiian Islands as well as the Mainland.

Today, the Stangas are in a great place. They love what they are doing. They have a 16,000 square foot facility which contains everything their business needs: laboratory, control room, growing rooms, offices, gift shop and room to host tours and events.

Currently, they are growing four varieties of mushrooms:

- **Alii** – Their number one seller, a mild-flavored mushroom.

- **Gray Oyster** – A meaty textured mushroom which goes great with fish or poultry.

- **Abalone** – A mushroom renowned for its flavor and health benefits.

- **Pioppini** – An Italian mushroom with bold taste which is popular with chefs and in Italian dishes.

They are in the enviable position of selling everything which they grow. They may expand their business by adding more outbuildings to grow additional mushrooms whereby they can increase distribution or begin to offer a new line of dehydrated mushrooms. Their product has even been served at an official state dinner at the White House. When noted Hawaiian Chef Alan Wong cooked at the Obamas' luau in 2009, he used Hamakua Mushrooms in the dinner.

Sure, they may be the only combination of helicopter pilot and interior designer mushroom farmers in the history of the universe, but Bob and Janice are living proof that even by going to where you least expect life to take you, you can make the most of it when you get there!

Hamakua Mushrooms Photo Album

Bob and Janice Stanga

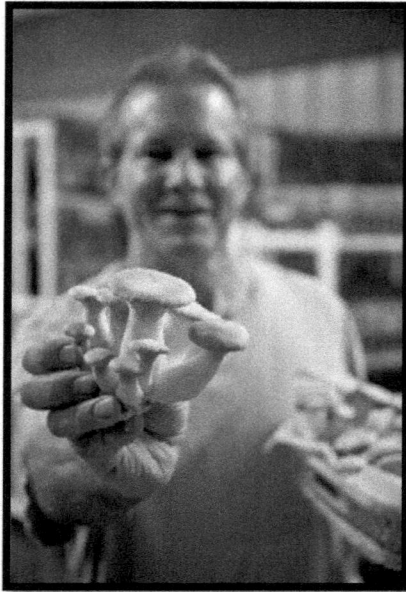

Bob showing one of Hamakua's Alii mushrooms

Visiting Hamakua Mushrooms is an interactive experience which includes a tour and education about mushrooms

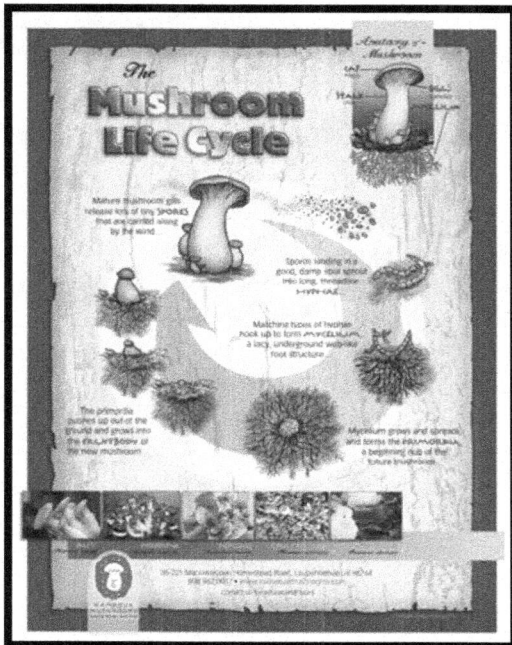

Some of the education from a Hamakua tour

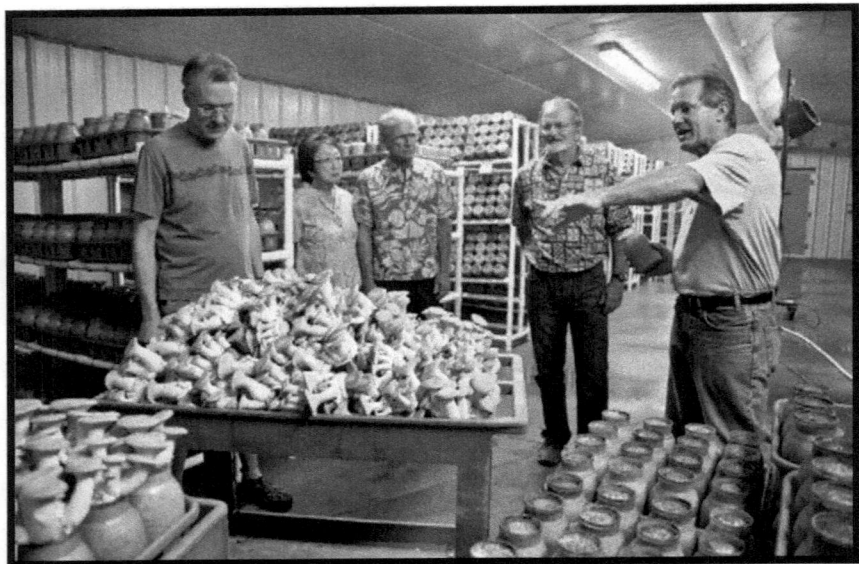
A stop at the growing room on a tour

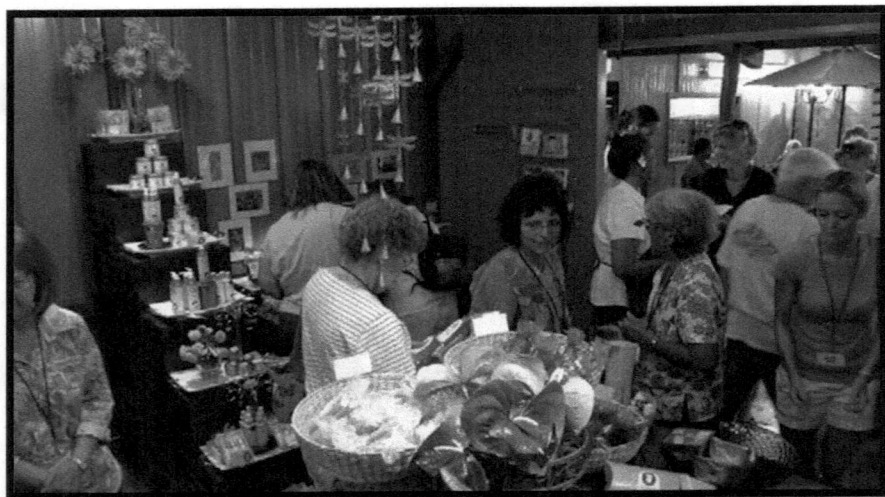
The gift shop at Hamakua Mushrooms

Mushroom products like their Maitake Mushrooms Green Tea

Hamakua Mushrooms' product lineup

Chapter 19: Passion Fruit
Aunty Liliko'i Products, LLC

9875 Waimea Road
Waimea, Kaua'i, HI 96796
(808) 338 - 1296

auntylilikoi.com
info@auntylilikoi.com

Established
1990

Leadership
Lori Cardenas, Owner

Products
Passion fruit-based food and personal care items

"At some point, we just decided let's see how far we can take the concept of using passion fruit in our products"...

The stereotypical story of the all-American couple goes like this:

> *Man and woman meet in high school. They fall in love and get married. They have two kids and are known as hard working "climb the company ladder," types who work their corporate jobs until retirement, where they then live out their golden years in a nice warm place.*
> *The End*

Lori and Tony Cardenas were right there:
- Met in high school – Check
- Fall in love/get married – Check
- Two kids – Check
- Hard working individuals with corporate jobs – Check

When you consider the fact they live on the Hawaiian Island of Kaua'i, it seems like the only thing keeping them from closing out this all-American tale was perhaps a few decades of work until retirement (clearly they have the "nice warm place" for their golden years sewed up with their home in Kaua'i).

Tony had a career in the defense industry and Lori had worked in a management capacity for a few different companies (manufacturing, fast food and lastly for a well-known Hawaiian-based t-shirt company). Lori's last stop had even afforded her the luxury of an ownership stake. Ultimately, she decided to leave the t-shirt industry and re-wrote their story entirely.

While she was searching for her next opportunity, she came across a small ad (2" x 2") in the *Garden Island*™, a local newspaper. The ad was seeking a new owner for Aunty Liliko'i Products.

She was not only familiar with Aunty Liliko'i as a local producer of passion fruit jellies, she even knew the owner, Tom Cassidy.

He had never mentioned he was going to be selling the company so she contacted him.

She was sad to hear that Tom was going to retire and move back to California. While she had been seeking a management position and not looking to run a business, she began to think about buying Aunty Liliko'i. She and Tony talked it over, and they decided with her skills in managing others' businesses, including the work from an ownership side from her time with the t-shirt company, she had the skill set she needed.

They decided to go for it!

They bought Aunty Liliko'i's which was literally nothing more than a name and five recipes. There was no inventory on hand, production plant, website or stash of supplies. The good news was the company had a great reputation for quality products, and the feedback on those five recipes was extremely positive. It was readily apparent Lori and Tony had something they could work with in Aunty Liliko'i.

The tie that bound all of Aunty Liliko'i's recipes together was passion fruit (liliko'i is the Hawaiian word for passion fruit). The flavorful, aromatic, and juicy fruity was a favorite of backyard gardeners in Hawai'i. While it does grow in frost-free climates like California and Florida in the United States, it is closely associated with Hawai'i and its culture. It is the perfect fruit for a product looking to be uniquely Hawaiian in spirit and taste.

While she was looking to expand the offerings she had, Lori decided to keep passion fruit as a key ingredient in all of the products Aunty Liliko'i produced. In fact, she wanted to push herself creatively to see how far she could take the concept of passion fruit.

Her line quickly began to expand from just jellies to barbecue sauces, mustards, syrups and dressings. She even added a personal care line with products like moisturizers, bubble bath, lip balm, etc.

Today she has more than 30 different items. While she adds variety by mixing in other flavors like pineapple, mango or guava, she has maintained her dedication to passion fruit, and it is still featured in every product.

Visitors to Hawai'i can find Aunty Liliko'i products at any number of retailers. The company has distribution in gift shops and grocery stores throughout the Islands and is even looking to further expand their presence in retail, having just hired a distributor to add even more accounts.

On their home base of Kaua'i, Aunty Liliko'i has a 2,200 square foot store. Visitors can see a production line of products cooling and getting labeled, or enjoy some samples while they shop for their favorite treats.

Lori has secured accounts on the Mainland, looking to add a taste of Hawai'i to their store shelves or on their menus. She even has some bars using some of her products in their signature drinks.

Individuals coming to Hawai'i might have a desire for Aunty Liliko'i's products before they arrive as she advertises in both Hawaiian Airlines'® and Alaskan Airlines'® in-flight magazines and many of the visitor publications.

Lori has used every bit of her 30+ years of management experience to assist in running her company. She is an early riser and typically spends 2 – 3 hours working at home before she heads into the store. It is in her home office where she handles accounting duties, paperwork and email. She then heads to the store for an eight-hour shift where she is involved in every facet of the company from cooking product to interacting with customers to calling on wholesale accounts.

She has three full-time employees and notes that working with them is the most rewarding aspect of owning her own company.

Keeping the company growing and profitable ensures not only her family makes a living but her employees as well.

The skills of their three employees allow them to do things which tend to be limited to much larger companies. She has a sales manager who is actively growing their wholesale business (currently, the company is split about 60% direct retail sales and 40% wholesale). They have a solid mail order business helmed by another employee, and they are also very active in social media, interacting directly with customers on Facebooks® and Twitter®.

Tony still works in the defense industry, but he helps out with the business as well. He maintains the website and assists with the layouts of their ads.

Lori continues to innovate with the passion fruit. Many of her ideas come from interacting with customers. She keeps track of customer suggestions, and if she hears multiple requests for a product, she tends to work on it to make it a uniquely Aunty Liliko'i product.

Her latest offering is available in-store only. She has a passion fruit cookie which is selling very well. She hasn't yet figured out how to ship a couple of jars of jelly with some cookies without ending up delivering a box of cookie crumbs so, at least for now, she's only offering cookies at the store.

Lori and Tony are at least 10 years from retirement. They aren't sure yet what they will do with Aunty Liliko'i when the time comes for them to quit working. Both of their sons live on the Mainland and are seemingly fairly established there (one is an airline pilot and the other is in the defense industry). They are a strong faith-based couple and know they will be given the answer with what to do when the time is right.

Tom Cassidy, the founder of Aunty Liliko'i, recently visited his daughter on Kaua'i for his 80th birthday. He took some time during his visit to meet with Lori while he was there. He had planned on leaving Hawai'i whether or not he found a new owner for the company. In his wildest dreams he wasn't able to imagine the heights which Lori and Tony have been able to get Aunty Liliko'i to reach. He simply couldn't have been happier for Lori and Tony for the great work they are doing with the brand.

It's true, Lori and Tony's vision and dedication seem to have the allure of an all-American success story!

Aunty Liliko'i Products Photo Album

The Cardenas family

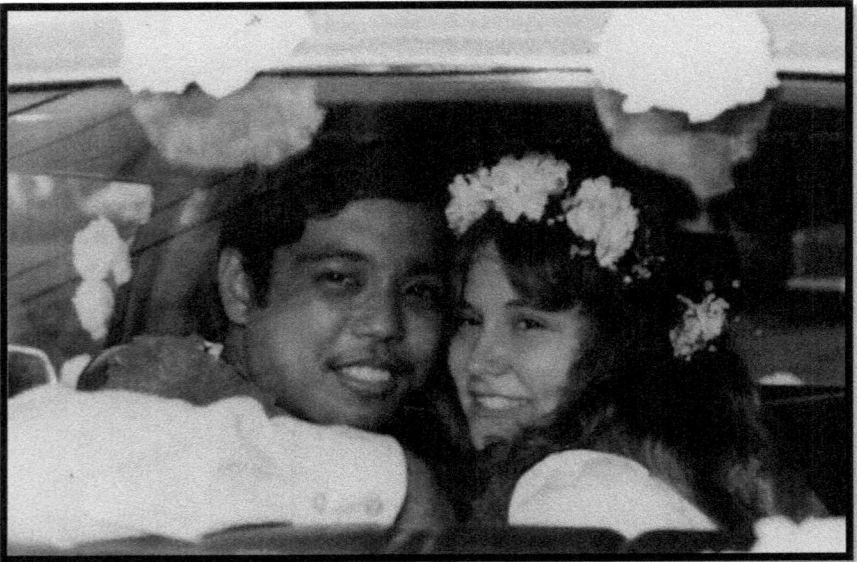

Tony and Lori on their wedding day

Passion fruit flower

Passion fruit

Aunty Liliko'i, the retail store

The original owner of Aunty Liliko'i, Tom Cassidy, visited for his 80th birthday

The Aunty Liliko'i team

Aunty Liliko'i product lineup

Chapter 20: Rum
Kōloa Rum Company

KŌLOA RUM CO. ™

DISTILLERS & BLENDERS

kaua`i · hawaii
3-2087 Kaumauli'i Highway
Lihue, Kaua'i, HI 96766
(808) 246 - 8900

koloarum.com
info@koloarum.com

Established
2006

Leadership
Bob Gunter, President and CEO

Products
Kōloa Rum and jams, jellies, syrups and drink mixes under the name Hawaiian Kukui

Helping bring back an industry which had thrived in Kaua'i for 173 years…

Sugarcane was first harvested commercially on Kaua'i in 1837. This wasn't the introduction of sugarcane to the island, though. The crew of Captain James Cook documented sugar cane growing when they landed on Kaua'i in 1778. This means it predated the arrival of the western world and was brought to the island by early Polynesian voyagers.

From 1837, all the way through 2010, sugarcane production was a large commercial industry on Kaua'i. With one final harvest in 2010, the Gay and Robinson Plantation shut down its operation, along with the last remnants of sugarcane production on the island.

The team at Kōloa Rum, with its name which is a Hawaiian word translating to "tall cane," understood the significance of this loss. Locally sourced sugarcane is the primary ingredient in their entire product line. In the short term, they bought up all of the Gay and Robinson Plantation final harvest they could get their hands on and put it into storage. In the long term, they were going to evaluate their entire business model.

Bob Gunter was born in South Carolina. He first came to Hawai'i when he was in the military. During his tour of duty in Vietnam, he enjoyed his R&R stint in Honolulu, vowing to come back to live permanently one day. After his discharge from the military, he actually settled in the San Francisco Bay area. He never forgot about his vow to get back to Hawai'i, though. Everything he was reading spoke about the booming sugarcane industry in Hawai'i. For Bob, it seemed like the perfect way to make the move.

With its 5 working sugarcane plantations, he settled on the island of Kaua'i. When the sugar industry started experiencing the issues which would lead to the aforementioned disappearance of all 5 sugarcane plantations on Kaua'i by 2010, Bob began to seek employment in a different industry.

As luck would have it, he got into the construction industry and two of the projects he worked on involved construction of distilleries. It seemed Hawai'i was going through a craft distillery renaissance, and he was gaining valuable and experience working on those projects.

Kōloa Rum was formed with a series of investors in 2006. From 2006 to 2008 they were busy securing permits and licensing for their company. During this time they were also able to make a purchase which would have a significant, positive impact on the organization. In December of 2007, the investors of Kōloa Rum purchased Hawaiian Kukui, an iconic brand in the area, which sold specialty products utilizing the local fruit to produce jams, jellies, syrups and drink mixes.

That company, started in 1931 by the Tateishi family, was going to be joining the Kōloa investor portfolio as an independently-run entity. This investment offered the luxury of space at its facility where the company's products were produced on Kaua'i. Later, they would open a tasting room and gift shop to showcase their Kōloa Rum (the product would be distilled offsite at a different facility 12 miles away at the Kilohana Plantation).

Needing an experienced professional to lead the construction of the new distillery, they hired Bob Gunter. Having already headed up distillery designs and build-outs in Maui, he brought the experience the Kōloa Rum team needed.

While they were working on building their distillery, visitor center/tasting room, they began to seek out the equipment they would need. Bob had some contacts in the industry from his work on his previous two jobs. He put out some feelers to see if anyone had a line of equipment suitable for their new company.

Soon they got some exciting news. Industry giant Brown-Forman® had decommissioned a huge copper still which had been built in 1947 by Liberty Coppersmith® in Philadelphia.

While most stills processed around 300 – 350 gallons of product at a time, this behemoth processed a whopping 1,210 gallons at a time! Bob Gunter traveled to Louisville to check it out. He ended up buying it on the spot, and they were officially in the distilled spirits business.

The year 2009 was significant for the company. They began bottling and selling their product, their distillery company store and tasting room was opened to the public, and they appointed Bob Gunter President and Chief Executive Officer.

Kōloa Rum felt like they had three distinct advantages over other companies in the distilled rum business:

1). The raw Hawaiian cane sugar sourced locally was better than the sugarcane found anywhere else in the world.

2). The company is lucky enough to be located near one of the wettest spots on the planet. About 450 – 500 inches of rainfall occurs in the local mountains. This water runs off, filters naturally through lava rock and flows down towards them. This water is some of the cleanest and best tasting water on the planet and is the second key ingredient in their product.

3). The modified antique copper still they purchased, complete with seven plates atop it, distills at a larger capacity than most competitors, and it delivers a smoother, higher proof product.

Using these three distinct advantages, the company began producing white, gold, dark, spice and eventually their all-natural coconut rum. Entering their products in international competitions, they garnered awareness in the industry as the accolades began to pile up.

A relationship with Hawaiian Airlines® also assisted the company in expanding beyond the Hawaiian Islands much quicker than they anticipated. The company offers their Kōloa White Rum as their "house rum" on its flights. They also offer their Kōloa's Ready-to-Drink Mai-Tai cocktail for anyone requesting this Hawaiian favorite. Hawaiian Airlines® also worked with Kōloa Rum to create a signature drink. The result became the Kōloa Breeze, a mixed drink containing rum, passion fruit, orange and guava, which they offer for free on flights going to-and-from Hawai'i and the U.S. Mainland.

The announcement the last sugarcane plantation on Kaua'i was closing was a tough one for the Kōloa Rum team. Their solution was simple: bring the industry back. While they used their back stock of sugarcane they loaded up on with the closing of the Gay & Robinson Plantation (augmenting it with sugarcane grown on Maui to stretch their stock), they continued to produce their product and started growing their own sugarcane. They planted their first 10 acres in 2012, which will be ready to harvest for their 2014 production. Their plan is to increase their sugarcane production to 50 acres over the next several years.

For those keeping score, the Kōloa Rum Company started in 2006, has managed to bring back an industry which was part of the life on Kaua'i for 173 years (sugarcane) and managed to save a 70+ year-old company which was considered by many to be a local treasure (their Hawaiian Kukui brand of locally-sourced fruit products). That's right, 243+ years of industry brought back/saved!

Today, visitors to the company's facility get to enjoy learning about the history of rum, sugarcane and the company. They can sample and shop for products.

Through connections made by Bob Gunter and the team at Kōloa Rum, and their name recognition through their affiliation with Hawaiian Airlines®, their product is not only available on the Mainland in the U.S. but in Canada, Australia and China. Clearly, there is a lot to be proud of with what the company is doing.

Bob Gunter is quick to point out that he's most proud of simply supporting and giving back to the local community. The team at Kōloa Rum is bringing jobs to the area. He quickly cites the fact

Kukui only had 4 employees when they purchased the company in 2007. Now they have 22 employees at the visitors center and the distillery.

Being that the company has already saved over 240 years of industry on the island, it's not hard to imagine their continued success for many years to come.

Kōloa Rum Photo Album

Bob Gunter

The star of the show: Kōloa Rum's 1,210 gallon copper still

Kōloa Rum's tasting room

Inside the tasting room

Kōloa Rum in its "natural" environment

Kōloa Rum's factory

Cheers!

Kōloa Rum's product lineup

Chapter 21: Salad Dressing
Hawaii's Special, Inc.

59-433 Kawowo Road
Haleiwa, O'ahu, HI 96712

(808) 256 - 3880

info@hawaiisspecial.com
hawaiisspecial.com

Established
2005

Leadership
David Delventhal, President

Products
Papaya seed dressing in four flavors: Original, Vinaigrette, Peppered Vinaigrette and Reduced Fat

"Being 'made in Hawai'i' does add some value and interest to your product, but it only goes so far. Offering a unique and quality salad dressing attracts new customers and brings repeat business."...

Dave Delventhal's father was a Lutheran school principal. As such, it is not uncommon to move around as you look to better yourself and seek new challenges. The "pre-internet" process to do this involved putting your name out there as someone seeking new opportunities, and church leaders would make you aware of what schools were searching for new administrators. You could then choose which of the schools you would like to speak to about an interview.

Dave's father seemed to be on the common path of moving every half-dozen years or so. He moved the family from Gary, Indiana when Dave was two to Colorado Springs, Colorado. It was a bit of a homecoming for the Delventhals as much of their family lived in the area. They only stayed six years until he began searching for a new opportunity.

He interviewed with schools in both California and Hawai'i. He ended up taking the job in Hawai'i on the Island of O'ahu. The plan was to be there 3 – 5 years. The family fell in love with the area and never moved again. Dave's father finished out his career there and retired in Hawai'i.

Dave didn't follow his father with a career in education. He connected with the outdoors and preferred a job outside the confines of an office building or classroom. He had studied to be a vet in college but elected to bypass it for a career and instead he became a commercial fisherman.

Over the course of a twenty-year fishing career, he moved twice. He had started near home, fishing off of the North Shore area of O'ahu. He then moved to Kaua'i before finishing out his last ten years of fishing based in Hilo on The Big Island. While he loved the work, twenty years of fishing takes a toll on your body. Dave began looking for a new opportunity. He knew he wanted to stick with a career where he could work outside without having to worry about the politics of an office job.

It seemed farming was the perfect solution for what he was seeking. He would still be able to be his own boss and work outside. The work, while still hard, would actually be easier than what he had been doing when he was fishing. He wasn't looking at this as a get-rich-quick scheme, but he thought the income would be more reliable and consistent over the ups-an-downs of fishing.

Since he was based in Hilo at the time, he thought the agriculture rich area of The Big Island would be the perfect place to start his farm. He took some classes at the Hilo campus of the University of Hawai'i. Before he made a move for a farm on The Big Island, he began to do some self-reflection. His family was on O'ahu. If he started a business there, not only would he be close to them, he would likely have less competition from other farmers than he would face on The Big Island.

It just made sense, so he moved back to O'ahu, the place where he grew up, and his family still lived. He continued to research farming, and in particular hydroponics farming on the internet. He also took a job at a farm to learn exactly what he would need to do to run his own business. After he was comfortable with his own skills, he rented some farmland and started growing head lettuce, cucumbers and tomatoes. He would sell his produce at the local farmers' markets.

His first commercial account came through a person he met who ran a lunch wagon. He wanted to know if Dave grew Spring Mix. He had a supplier in California, but the quality was very inconsistent. He thought sourcing it locally could rectify the issues he had been experiencing. Dave agreed to start growing this greens mixture on the spot. Luckily, he would later find he could have a solid income-producing harvest of Spring Mix on about an acre of land.

Soon, Dave was selling head lettuce and Spring Mix to about 70% of the restaurants in the North Shore portion of O'ahu. His success afforded him the luxury of being able to secure his own farm. He named it Pupukea Gardens.

In addition to selling to local restaurants, Dave had continued to sell at farmers' markets. He supplemented his produce sales by selling mixed salads for shoppers to dine on while they were there.

Offering fresh salads creates the need for salad dressing. Rather than offering store-bought brands, Dave's Mom suggested he use her unique papaya seed dressing she had always made for the family. Dave thought it was a great idea and his customers did too. They immediately not only wanted dressing for their salads, they wanted to buy it by the cup to take home with them.

Soon, Dave was bottling his dressing under the name Pupukea Gardens and selling it to both his farmers' market customers and his wholesale lettuce customers. In 2003, his salad dressing business grew beyond what he could create onsite at the farm so he acquired a commercial kitchen. As business continued to expand, he decided to separate the salad dressing business from the farm so he incorporated the dressing under the name Hawaii's Special, Inc. in 2005.

As he gained more customers, he began getting requests to expand the product line beyond simply the original formula. His first expansion came through individuals seeking a healthier dressing, so he took out the sugar and changed the vinegar from regular to apple cider vinegar, and then he had a Papaya Seed Vinaigrette.

The next incarnation of the dressing came from a fiery foods show in Albuquerque he attended for a few years. His interaction with the individuals there led him to add a Peppered Vinaigrette to the mix. Finally, he added a reduced fat version of the original which added xanthan gum to give the dressing a creamy consistency.

While Dave has a large presence on O'ahu and has distributors securing shelf space for him on the other islands in Hawai'i, the future of the company seems embedded in one of two markets: Japan or the U.S. Mainland. The upside is tremendous for each, and Dave does have minimal presence in both right now. Despite the daunting process of dealing with paperwork and regulations involving shipping to another country, Japan seems to have the edge at the moment.

While each involves the cost of shipping long distance overseas, Japan seems to have gained the advantage through some publicity Dave has received there. Features in various publications have started to build up a demand for Hawaii's Special in Japan. It's fairly common for tourists from Japan to come over with a list of popular items to seek out while visiting. These are brands which are popular in the market but have limited availability there. Hawaii's Special has become a "list item" for many Japanese visitors.

This designation has helped in creating enough of an interest in the product, and it is apparent Dave has some inroads with some retailers. There are many obstacles to overcome still, but he is working with a distributor now and could see an expanded distribution in Japan in the near future.

Without the same sort of exposure in the United States, he's been left trying to get into the Mainland as a largely unknown entity. Without consumers demanding stores carry Hawaii's Special, he's trying to navigate a playing field set-up for much larger brands to excel. The small brand is often shut out with the various warehouse slotting fees, ad fees and shelf fees. It's almost impossible for any small brand to break through the system, much less someone trying to do so from as far away as Hawai'i. He has been left to penetrate the Mainland market through his mail-order business.

Still, Dave has left the door open to break into the U.S. Mainland market via conventional distribution at a later time. He's open to any ideas/partnerships to get there. Under the right circumstances he might even consider a manufacturing facility on the Mainland which would get him over two of his largest hurdles: the cost of shipping in raw materials and shipping his product out of Hawai'i.

Dave loved his time as a commercial fisherman, but owning his farm and a salad dressing company has been even more rewarding. He gets the joy of interacting with customers and hearing directly from consumers how much they like his products. Dave recently found a person to take over Pupukea Gardens which will allow him to focus exclusively on his salad dressing business. He hopes to be able to take his dressing business to the next level by being able to give it his full-time attention.

Over time, he hopes that building up his salad dressing business will do something he wasn't able to get as a fisherman: a retirement. While he's not stopping anytime soon, if he can continue the upward trajectory he's been on as a part-time business, he should do well and continue to build equity in a company which should offer value to a buyer down the road.

It appears Dave has already figured out the key to the success of his brand moving forward. He doesn't have the marketing dollars, the distribution channels or the staff to take the approach the nationally known large companies utilize for their products. His avenue to success is going to be through offering a unique and high quality product. That first, and perhaps most important step of building a brand is checked off of his list. Plus, he has the sexiness of being created in Hawai'i using locally-sourced ingredients and he has a product backed by the guidance and enthusiasm of Dave Delventhal.

Sounds likes it's only a matter of time before everybody knows what's so special about Hawaii's Special!

Hawaii's Special, Inc. Photo Album

Dave Delventhal

Dave at Pupukea Gardens

Dave during his time as a commercial fisherman

Dave works with local artist Mark Swanson
(*alohaworkshop.com*) to custom design the retro-cool artwork
on his bottles

Salad dressing production

Dave showing off his products

These 5 ½ oz. bottles which appeal to the tourist trade

Hawaii's Special product lineup (including new offerings Dave is just now coming out with)

Chapter 22: Salad Dressing
Minato Hawaii

961 Akepo Lane
Honolulu, HI 96817
(808) 781 - 5916

minatohawaiiangift.com
mac@minatohawaiiangift.com

Established
1980

Leadership
Mac Takeda, Owner

Products
Salad dressings, seasonings, barbecue sauce, handmade soaps and almond brittle

Take a taste of Hawai'i home with you...

There are different reasons to get into the restaurant business. For some, it's the allure of fusing ingredients and experimenting with flavors. Others like to offer family recipes to the public. Some see it simply as a business and a means to be self-employed.

Mac Takeda loves working with food, and it's always been rewarding for him to meld traditional Japanese dishes and American cuisine in his restaurants, but the true reason he got into the business: he's a people person.

He loves to interact, entertain and learn about people. His restaurants have been a conduit to entering into customers' lives... even if it's just for the span of a visit for lunch or dinner.

Mac Takeda was born in Tokyo. His first taste of the business occurred when he was in college. McDonald's® was just starting to come to Japan. To say he loved the work was an understatement. His positive attitude, willingness to work hard and his stellar customer service made him a standout employee with management, including the U.S. representatives from McDonald's® headquarters who were often on-hand overseeing the company's entrance to this important new market.

He was such a go-getter and company guy, he got the nickname "Mac" (short for McDonald's®) which is what he is known exclusively as today. One of the corporate executives thought it would be a great learning experience for Mac to spend a year working at a U.S. location. There he would be able to experience how a domestic McDonald's® operates, and he could bring back some of the best practices to his store in Tokyo.

Mac was more than willing to spend a year working and going to school abroad, especially when they offered to allow him to work at the Waikiki McDonald's®. He had visited Hawai'i with his family while he was in high school and really enjoyed his time there.

After a thoroughly enjoyable year in Hawai'i, Mac went back to Japan to complete his college degree and continue to work at McDonald's® in Tokyo. It looked like he would stay on with McDonald's® in a management capacity, helping build the brand in Asia.

He put those plans on hold, though, to visit the United States. His goal was to explore the U.S. to look into the idea of going to graduate school somewhere in the United States.

After traveling across the U.S., Mac found a place which felt like home for him. He found a large Japanese community in San Jose, California. He looked at San Jose State University but changed his plans again when he heard about a restaurant in San Jose where the owner would assist employees in securing a green card to stay in the United States if they worked in his restaurant for two years.

Mac's new plan was to work in the restaurant for two years, get his green card, and then go to San Jose State University.

It didn't happen, though.

Well, not all of it anyway. Mac did work his two years at the restaurant, and the owner did help him secure his green card. As much as he had loved McDonald's®, Mac loved a full-service restaurant even more. Once again, it was all about the people. Interacting with them, seeing them out for a dinner and having a good time, it was just all fun and exciting for him.

In 1980, rather than go back to school, Mac opened Minato's, his own Japanese/American cuisine restaurant. Opening in 1980 meant he was getting started right as the tech companies were getting rolling in the area. Over the years Mac literally had the who's who of Silicone Valley (including Steve Jobs) dine at his restaurant.

Mac helped set Minato's apart from the other Japanese restaurants in the area by offering diners a line of salads. He had noticed individuals often sought the healthy option of dining on salads in other restaurants, but most Japanese restaurants didn't have salads. Those that did typically had the same miso-based-dressings (the traditional Japanese seasoning).

In addition to simply offering salads, Mac further differentiated himself by offering unique dressings he prepared onsite himself. It didn't take long for customers to discover these homemade dressings. Soon they were demanding Mac sell them some of his salad dressing so they could use it at home.

He wasn't set-up to offer packaged dressing so when he would relent, he put it in a cup for them to take home. This continued all the way until 2000 when Mac decided to move his restaurant to Honolulu. Twenty years in one location was long enough, and he had longed to get back to Hawai'i after spending the year there working at McDonald's® and going to school.

A change in scenery didn't change what Mac's customers thought about his salad dressings. Just like in San Jose, they wanted the opportunity to purchase his dressings to take home.

Rather than continuing to send customers home with cups of dressing, Mac started preparing and bottling his dressings in his kitchen. His plan was to just offer it onsite to his customers, but when the word got out he was bottling his dressing, stores began to call him.

He decided to go all out and try to sell his product wholesale. It wasn't long before he was hustling to prepare salad dressing, make sales calls and deliver his product, while he had a successful restaurant to maintain as well.

By 2006, Mac had two full-time jobs with his two businesses. He decided to sell his restaurant, open a factory to make his dressing and see how far he could take his wholesale food business.

He knew to be successful he would need to expand beyond the stores around Minato's Restaurant and the Japanese grocery stores in which he was currently selling his product. One chain he really had his eye on was the ABC® stores which dominate the convenience stores for both tourists and locals in Hawai'i.

Initially he wasn't having a lot of luck getting into ABC®. It seemed he was suffering from the "chicken and the egg" syndrome. Store managers have authority to decide what products go into the stores they are responsible for managing. He kept getting turned away because he wasn't in any other ABC Stores®. It wasn't clear how you could get into a store because he couldn't get past the fact every manager wanted to know in which of the ABC Stores® he had representation.

The grocery business is notoriously a tough business to crack. It's not uncommon to hear about the "wars of grocer's shelves" over the real estate to sell manufacturer's products. Well, all is fair in love and war so Mac got a little sneaky.

When Mac got his dressing into the hands of a corporate-level buyer at ABC®, he never heard back from him. He decided to take matters into his own hands by placing ads in tourist magazines, appealing to Japanese travelers to Hawai'i. The magazines he targeted were printed in Japanese. He bought ads which featured his product and had the tagline, "Available at ABC Stores®."

These Japanese nationals, most unable to speak English, would take these magazines to ABC® looking for Minato Hawai'i salad dressings. They would point to the ads asking for it. The confused employees and managers (they couldn't read the ad copy) began to call Mac asking him to start selling his dressing in their stores since they had a demand for it.

Brilliant!

Once he cracked ABC®, other large retailers quickly followed. Soon he was in Costco®, Wal-Mart®, and the Dole Plantation®. He even got a deal with Japan Airlines®, offering his dressing on all flights Hawai'i to Japan. When the company had some financial difficulties, it looked like he might lose his affiliation with the company. It turned out to be a blessing, though. Japan Airlines® sold off its catering division to another company which services every other major airline out of Honolulu. The new catering company offers Mac's dressings on every airline they service on flights between Hawai'i and Asia.

The salad dressing business is going great for Mac. He misses the restaurant business, though. Speaking with customers is something he really misses and craves. His interaction with individuals outside of his company is pretty limited these days. He is tied-up managing his business for the most part. He has figured out a way to get out of the office and foster conversation. He actually services the ABC® stores in the tourist areas around Waikiki himself. The stores open between 6:30 and 7:00 a.m. He can park on the street with his commercial vehicle until 8:30 a.m. so Mac starts many days "meeting and greeting" ABC® store managers, employees and customers.

Those face-to-face conversations are what he craves. So much so, he is looking forward to a time when he can own and operate his own restaurant again.

If you ever are visiting Honolulu, and you are in an ABC® store early in the morning and you see someone filling the shelves with Minato Hawai'i Salad Dressings, it's probably Mac Takeda. Be sure to say hi. He'd like that!

Also, do yourself a favor while you are there; pick up a bottle of his dressing. You will not only have a new friend for life, you will have a new favorite salad dressing as well.

Mac Takeda

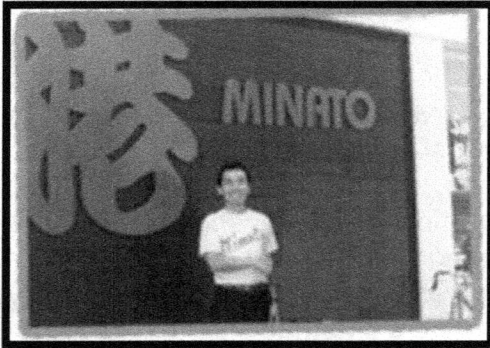

Mac outside of his original Minato restaurant in California

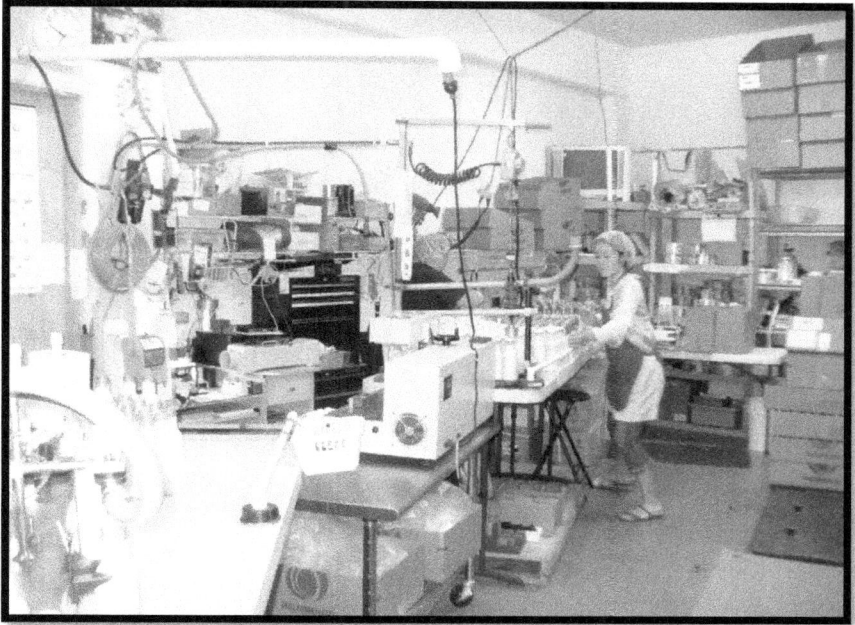
Bottle line in the production facility

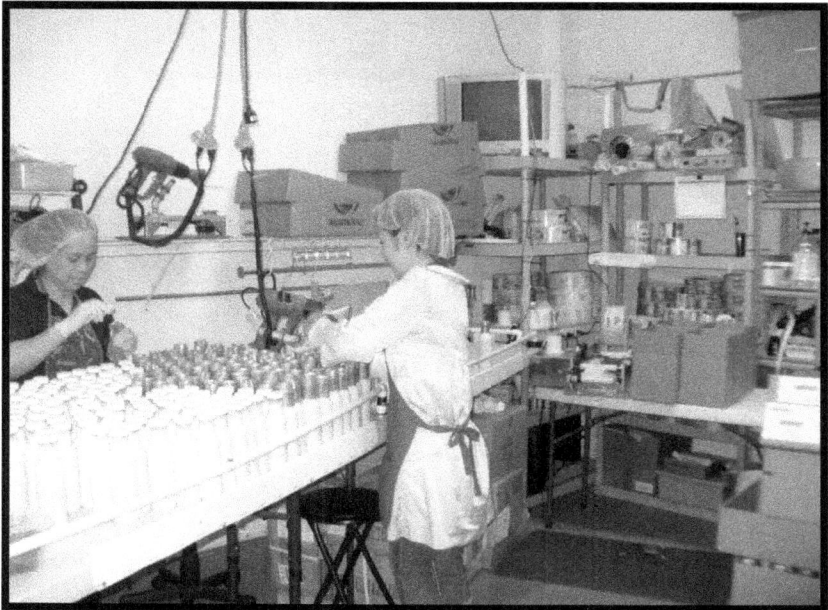
Making Minato Hawaii Salad Dressing

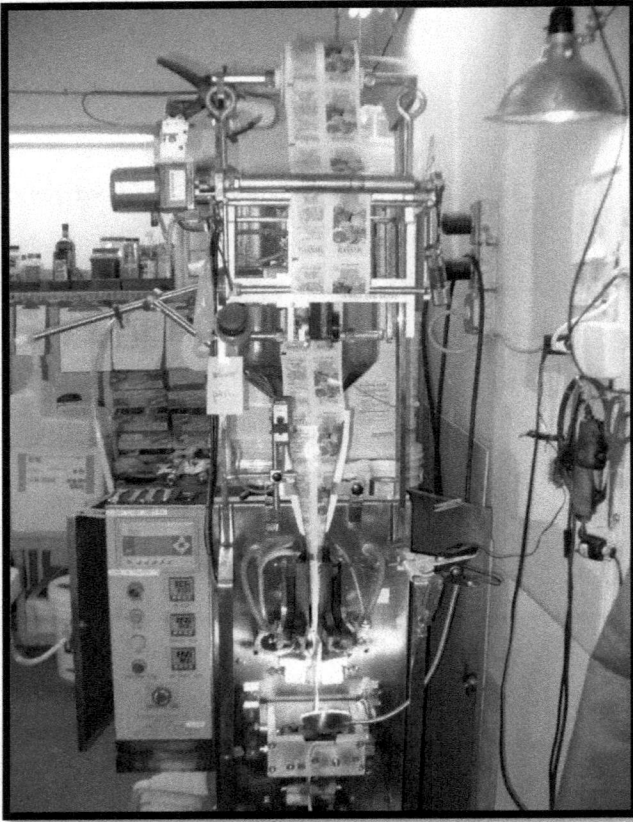
Labeling station

Mac's mascot is a cartoon pineapple

Sample of label detail

Minato Hawaii product lineup

Chapter 23: Soap
Kona Natural Soap

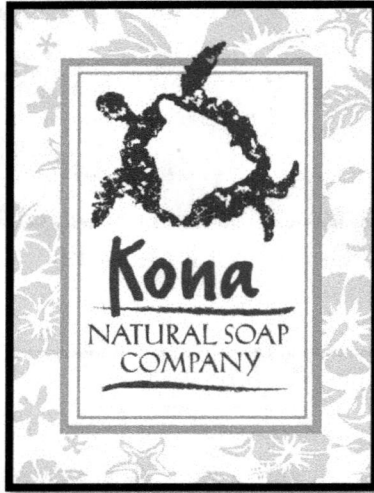

P.O. Box 391114
Keauhou, Hawai'i, HI 96739
(808) 322 - 9111

konanaturalsoap.com
konasoap@aol.com

Established
2005

Leadership
Greg Colden, Soap Maker & CEO
Marty Corrigan, CFO

Products
Natural soaps, 100% Kona coffee, kukui nut oil and cocoa
beans

Brought to you by the American Council of Paradigm Shifts...

Greg Colden is a big proponent of the paradigm shift. When life deals you the mundane, don't keep doing what you've always done, just because you've always been doing it. Too many of us fall into the trap of continuing on with life when we are miserable, just because it's the path of least resistance.

Even though Greg likes to talk about the need for a paradigm shift, he knows how difficult it can be. He found himself falling into the trap of needing to make a change, but struggling to put together a plan to help get him released from a life where his happiness had taken a backseat to the responsibilities of the life, he, and his partner Marty Corrigan, had built for themselves.

Greg was born in Los Angeles. As an adult, he moved to San Francisco where he worked in management at a law firm. While working there, he was recruited to manage an insurance company. He found a calling when he started selling insurance, while managing the operation. Initially he was selling lines of personal insurance, and then he decided to jump fully into insurance and opened his own office.

After many years managing a record store, Marty also joined the insurance industry. He started out in underwriting and ended up moving into management on the financial side where his attention to detail from underwriting paid off (which it still continues to do to this day for Kona Natural Soap).

From an outsider's perspective, they had a really great life. Excellent jobs which afforded them the luxury of being able to travel, which had become a passion for them.

Despite the enviable life they were living, Greg and Marty believed there was something different they could/should be doing. Greg truly started to believe there was more to life than his name on the side of an insurance building he owned.

At the same time this yearning for trying something else, four unique circumstances came together in a very short timeframe which became the accelerator for their paradigm shift, resulting in a new life and business for them in Hawai'i.

The first two events to lead to their new life happened on trips to Hawai'i. Greg and Marty went to visit some friends and go snorkeling. Greg was badly burned on an overcast day while being out all afternoon without wearing a shirt. He ended up in an enlightening moment when he bathed with a nationally known company's "natural" soap. It turned out there really wasn't anything "natural" about the product at all. In fact, it intensified his pain as it removed a layer of skin.

Marty suggested they could do a better job making a natural soap. He suggested the two of them give it a whirl. Greg wasn't so sure, but Marty would eventually get a book detailing soap making, and Greg would become hooked on the idea.

They ended up finding a local woman near their home who made soap. Between the book, the hands-on training offered by the local woman, and Greg's own laser-like obsessive focus, he was fully hooked on soap making. Greg isn't the type to ever get into something halfway. When he's in, he's going full bore. It's exactly what he was doing with his soap making. Not only was he seeking out the best ingredients, he needed to know all of the science behind soap making as well. A simple recipe of "heat this" and "add this, let cool" wasn't enough for him. He had to know why various agents bonded together, or why certain ingredients reacted well with each, but not others, etc.

Initially, Greg was thinking his paradigm shift was going to happen in retirement. While in Hawai'i, they met with a real estate agent friend whom they spoke to about their retirement. They gave her some basic parameters for their dream situation to live out their retired years among the beauty of The Big Island in Hawai'i. The marching orders for their friend were to take her time, they were probably 10 – 20 years from making the move, but when the perfect scenario came about to let them know. They could even foresee making the move a year or so early if the situation was just right.

Though they didn't know it, getting into soap making, and inquiring about a place to retire to in Hawai'i would be the start of their big change. With the visions of retirement in his head, Greg, an avid reader, picked up the book, **So You Want to Live in Hawai'i.** He thought it would be a good Saturday read wrought with tips to help him out when the time was just right to head south to Hawai'i. As he read the book, the idea of moving to Hawai'i right then started sounding better and better. The words seemed to speak to him to not wait until the perfect scenario, but instead to make the time right for himself now.

The final component fell into place when Greg went back to his job. He fielded a call from someone who wanted to purchase his insurance business. Not someone just window shopping either; a true opportunity to sell out.

As he took a few days to marinate on the idea of selling his business, the phone rang again. It was his real estate agent. She had the ultimate place for Greg and Marty. Exactly what they were looking for, a farm on The Big Island and the price was right.

Let's see…
- ✓ A new hobby in soap which could translate to a new business in Hawai'i; way more laid back and way more fun than the insurance business.

- ✓ A chance to own a farm on The Big Island, just where they wanted to be in a picturesque and perfect setting.

- ✓ The ideas from the book made it seem not as arduous as he thought to make the move; in fact, it made it seem imperative he make the move as soon as possible.

✓ A solid offer to buy out his business; clearly one of the biggest sticking points stopping him from going.

Sometimes life helps you make decisions. With all of this coming together at the same time, it seemed crazy not to make the move. With sadness for his employees, Greg handed out some bonus checks and announced he was selling the company, his home in Oakland, and he and Marty were moving to Hawai'i to open a natural soap business.

The land in Hawai'i had some cacao trees, some coffee trees and a few old mango trees. The rest they would need to build themselves. The first thing Greg and Marty did was build a duplex on the property (before they even moved there). This wasn't to be their home long-term, but offered a great place to stay while their soap factory and home were being built on the farm.

Building in Hawai'i was difficult, especially early on when they were back-and-forth between Oakland and The Big Island. Once they were able to focus on the business, the Kona Natural Soap Company was born. Marty designed the logo and the website. He would also handle the shipping for their internet orders. His meticulous approach to packaging every order would become a signature of the company (you have to place an order just to see how Marty places everything together, building compartments in the shipping boxes and tying things together perfectly).

Greg's job was to make the soap. It's a fairly intricate process which involves creating a solution of rainwater and sodium hydroxide the night before. He begins by adding palm kernel oil and coconut oil (which creates the lather of the soap) and heating them slowly. He introduces extra virgin olive oil, pours in the rainwater/sodium hydroxide mixture, and then he puts it in mixer, turns it off, turns it back on again, etc., until the two properties are blended to the point of being soap.

Finally, when it starts to thicken, he adds kukui nut oil and the "essential oils" which provide the aromatherapy of his soap and the components to the mix that make it uniquely Kona Natural Soap, like ground papaya seeds, ground citrus seeds, ground rosemary leaves or 100% Kona coffee. The soap is then insulated in plastic for 72 hours before being allowed to rest for a week. After that time, it is ready to cut and box for sale.

Greg and Marty have been able to grow their business organically one customer at a time. Greg's commitment to his craft, using the finest locally-sourced ingredients possible, has made for a product with repeat business. Individuals who try their product often become customers for life, discarding their reliance of the well-known megabrands.

Giving away samples (small sliver bars) has been a key marketing initiative to introduce customers to their product. People are often amazed when they are looking at their soaps, and they are given a bar to try. Certainly, there is a cost to doing this, but more often than not, Greg and Marty not only have a customer for life, they have a new friend.

One of the most rewarding parts of this endeavor has been getting to know so many new people. They are able to be introduced to new experiences through their customers. Greg points out when people come to Hawai'i, they tend to be in a great mood. They are in a beautiful place, away from the drudgery of work, and the distractions and stresses of home. They like the fact they are meeting people at their very best.

In addition to giving out samples, Greg and Marty have also built up their clientele by participating in two different tours offered by local companies. They are part of a local agriculture tours where their farm is showcased and part of a house tour where they welcome visitors to their home. The visitors then enjoy the first course of a three-course meal on their lana'i.

Their most popular soap is one called Nani Lemi. It's a great facial cleanser made with lime and lime seeds, though it gives off a slightly lemony bouquet. Most of the concoctions (regular and seasonal) Greg comes up with seem to find an audience. He's had only one exception. He thought it might be a good idea to create an unscented version for those suffering from allergies. It never sold, and they ended up giving it out as gifts.

Greg no longer even thinks about a paradigm shift in his life. He is doing exactly what he wants to do. The only goal he and Marty have now is to keep doing what they are doing until they can't do it anymore. They live in Hawai'i and get to meet awesome new people who love a product they create. It always means the world to Greg and Marty when they hear from satisfied customers or individuals who suffer from skin allergies, telling them how much their product has positively impacted their lives. What's not to love about that?

Yes, it's been a complete change for the better for Greg and Marty. Greg likes to reflect on an incident which occurred around the time he took up soap making, they found their farm, he read the book about moving to Hawai'i and his business was sold. Everything was already in motion. The farm was purchased, and his business was transitioning to new owners.

A man came in wearing a sarong with long, dirty dreadlocks. His staff was frightened so they had Greg do the consultation himself. When Greg began talking to the man, the customer informed him he was from Hawai'i. When Greg shared the fact he had bought a farm in Keauhou on The Big Island, the man said, "Ah, you must be connected to the earth. The thinnest crust of magma found anywhere in the world is right there. Those who are connected to the earth are drawn there." When you look at it like that, maybe, just maybe, Greg and Marty's life in Hawai'i is actually bigger than a paradigm shift.

It might just have been their destiny!

Kona Natural Soap Photo Album

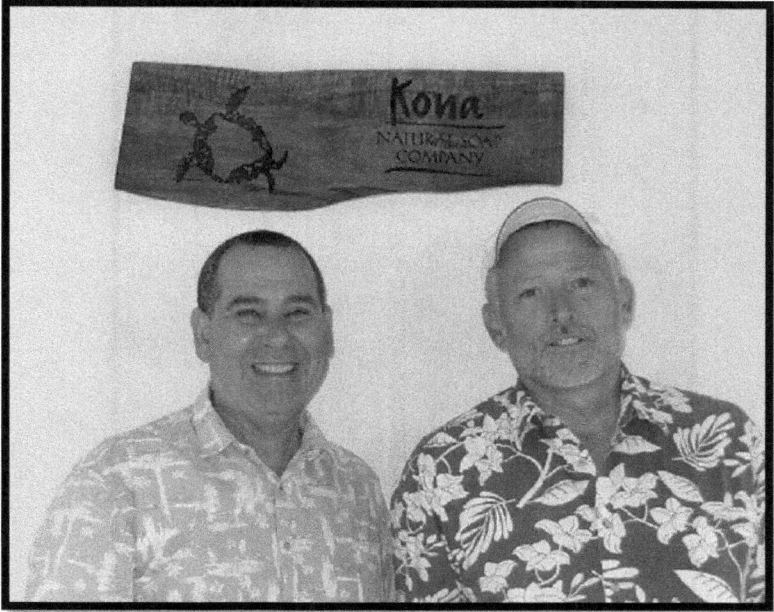

Greg Colden and Marty Corrigan

Soap samples

Greg making soap

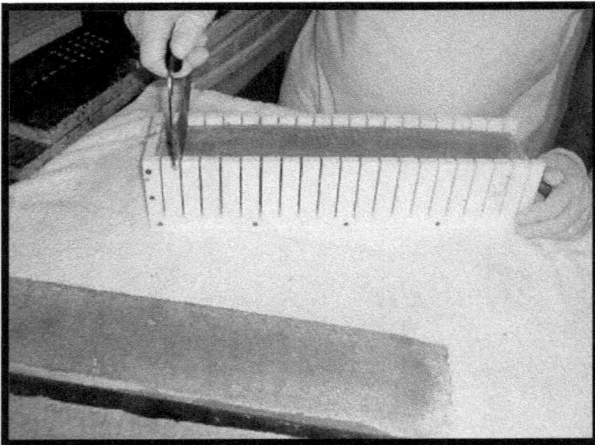

Cutting soap into bars

Kona Natural Soap Company's product lineup includes roasted cocoa beans, coffee and kukui nut oil

Kona Natural Soap Company's soap lineup

Chapter 24: Spices
Aloha Spice Company

3857 Hanapepe Road
Hanapepe, Kaua'i, HI 96716
(808) 335 - 5960

alohaspice.com
info@alohaspice.com

Established
2007

Leadership
Joanna Carolan, Owner

Products
Herbs, seasonings, rubs, spices and sugars

Even the product lineup says "Aloha"…

When Joanna Carolan was 8-years-old, her grandparents moved to Kaua'i . Her grandfather, a psychiatrist by trade, was near the end of his career. He was looking ahead towards retirement when a colleague informed him of the opportunity to run a psychiatric hospital on Kaua'i . He had always wanted to run a hospital, so he couldn't pass up this chance to fulfill a lifelong dream. Plus, the move to Hawai'i meant he would be in a place which would be perfect for his retirement.

During a visit their first year in Kaua'i , Joanna declared it was so beautiful she would one day move there herself and create a business where "people can paint." Little did Joanna's family know that it would take her a few decades, but this dream would eventually come true.

Her family resided in the San Francisco Bay area, but they would frequently go to visit her grandparents, and she continued to love staying there. During her early teenage years, she began to get into a bit of trouble at home. Her parents finally determined she needed to get away from the crowd she was hanging with at home, so at the age of 14 she was sent to live with her grandparents in Hawai'i.

From an outsider's perspective, being forced to move to Hawai'i didn't seem like much of a "punishment." She ended up enjoying living there full-time and managed to keep out of trouble. She stayed throughout her high school years, and after graduation she headed back to the Mainland.

In college she studied English literature. During those college years she had an uncle with a sailboat who would often get her to join him on his adventures. She enjoyed sailing trips through the Caribbean, the Galapagos and New Guinea.

These tropical trips sparked her desire to get back to Hawai'i. In 1990, she moved to Kaua'i with a goal of selling artwork in gift stores. Through cold-calling she was making inroads in getting her work in store by store when tragedy struck the island. In September of 1992, Hurricane Iniki struck Kaua'i directly. This was the most devastating hurricane in the history of Hawai'i.

The damage throughout the island meant the gift shops weren't open and couldn't sell her artwork. She gave up on her business and started working on the rebuilding efforts of the island. As she entered the construction industry, she began painting tiles, and the homeowners seemed to really like her work.

She even developed a signature tile she would put in all of the homes she worked on. It is customary to remove your shoes upon entering a home in Hawai'i. Her tile simply stated, "Please remove your shoes. Mahalo!" The homeowners so liked these whimsical little tiles she began to think that once the island began to recover, and things got back to normal, she could resume her art business by selling painted tiles.

That is exactly what she did. In 1996 she began creating a series of Hawaiian-themed artworks on tile, and it became her flagship product line. Unlike the slower turns of original artwork in the gift stores, her tiles were constant turns and cash register rings in the stores she partnered with.

Her business continued to grow rapidly until 2002. It was then she noticed a new competitor in the market. This new competitor was using similar designs to hers with one big difference: the tiles weren't manufactured in Hawai'i, they were manufactured in China!

While there are certainly plenty of tourists and locals looking to buy handmade products created and made in Hawai'i, there are also a large faction of individuals who simply shop price. Joanna knew she couldn't compete on price with goods manufactured in China.

Although she had taken a bit of a hit with the competitor featuring goods from China, she had simply lost market share.

She still had a viable business on her hands with the painted tiles, but she just thought it would probably be a good time to diversify. It was apparent she could easily become the victim of "too many eggs in one basket" if she didn't develop something else to offer her valued gift shop partners.

For her new business, she wanted to do something totally different, yet keep to something she knew as well. She decided to go with spices. Her father had been in the restaurant business for his entire career, and she believed it would be a nice tribute to him for her to also enter the food industry. Plus, she liked the idea of developing a line of spices/seasonings/rubs which carried on the traditions of Hawaiian cooking. The best part was she would be able to use the distribution channels she already had in place with the tile business to sell this new product line.

She worked with local Chef Michael Simpson to develop flavor profiles utilizing locally harvested products. These blends would be mixed by hand, and feature organic, and locally grown goods whenever possible. Chef Simpson also helped her create a cookbook with recipes featuring the product line they had created.

The product line included seasonings, rubs and sugars. Twists on local favorites like rubs containing locally grown coffee were included.

They even borrowed from a favorite they saw on the Mainland: smoked salts. Using a locally non-native and invasive fruit wood (Strawberry Guava), they smoked their sea salts to give them a uniquely Hawaiian taste. Harvesting a non-native and invasive tree seemed to keep with the "aloha spirit" they were seeking with the company. It helped the land, and it made their product bold and unique to them.

The Aloha Spice Company's product line even says "Aloha". Check it out:

Aloha Spice Cookbook

Lovely Gift Sets

Organic Seasonings and Rubs

Hawaiian Sea Salts/Grinders

Aromatic Sugar and Spice

Thus far, Joanna's diversification strategy is working out well. She was put to the test with a tough economy in 2008/2009. While she saw a dip in tile sales, which makes sense with consumer limiting discretionary spending, she saw her spice business continue to grow. People still needed to eat, and it even appeared as though they were eating out less to save money. Then perhaps they were trying to make their stay-at-home meals a little bit more fun by spicing them up with her products.

Today, she runs two separate businesses. Banana Patch Studio (*bananapatchstudio.com*) is the business name for her tile company which she distributes via gift stores and hotels. It also has a physical location where customers can buy her tiles as well as her original artwork. Joanna is an accomplished artist with her work hanging all over Hawai'i (her latest project was multiple murals for the Marriott® in Waikiki). Banana Patch Studio is also a working studio where the artists Joanna has hired are not only painting the tiles she designs, but also offering their own artwork as well.

A place so beautiful with a business where people can come and paint? It seems 8-year-old Joanna saw this coming a long time ago.

Right next door to Banana Patch Studio is the Aloha Spice Company. Like the tile business, Aloha Spices are available via gift shops throughout the Hawaiian Islands and at her retail store. Joanna not only offers her complete product line at her

Aloha Spice Company retail store but other locally made products as well. It's a rewarding aspect of her company in being able to introduce others to locally made products in addition to her own. Plus, she knows the trials and tribulations of knocking on doors trying to get store owners to try your products so it's fun for her to be the person giving business owners a chance to sell their product at retail in her store.

Hanapepe is an "independent town" in that it was on the outskirts of a sugar plantation and not affiliated with the plantation. When the sugar cane producers closed down, many of these independent towns shut down as well. Hanapepe has continued to thrive as it became a town renowned as an artists' community as they began to move in as rents became lower.

Joanna Carolan is an artist who is giving back to a community she has loved for a long time!

Aloha Spice Company Photo Album

Joanna Carolan

Aloha Spice Company store

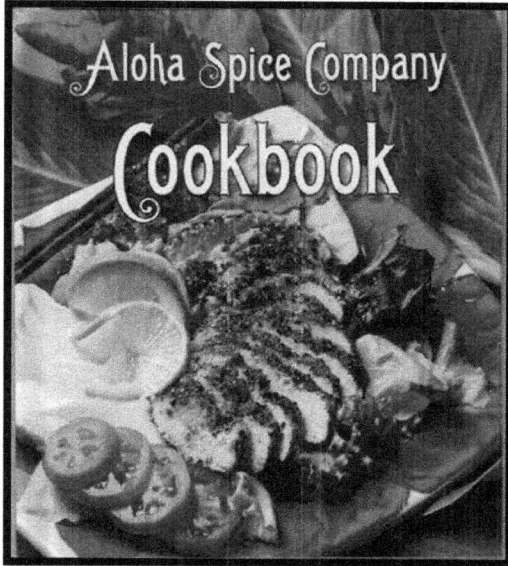

The Aloha Spice Company Cookbook contains recipes highlighting the company's spices and blends

Banana Patch Studio is Joanna's other business; it features her tiles and original artwork

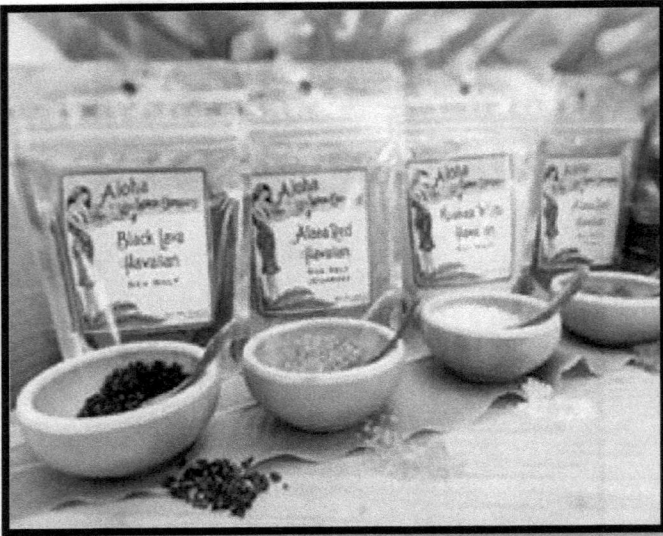
Aloha Spice Company specialty salts

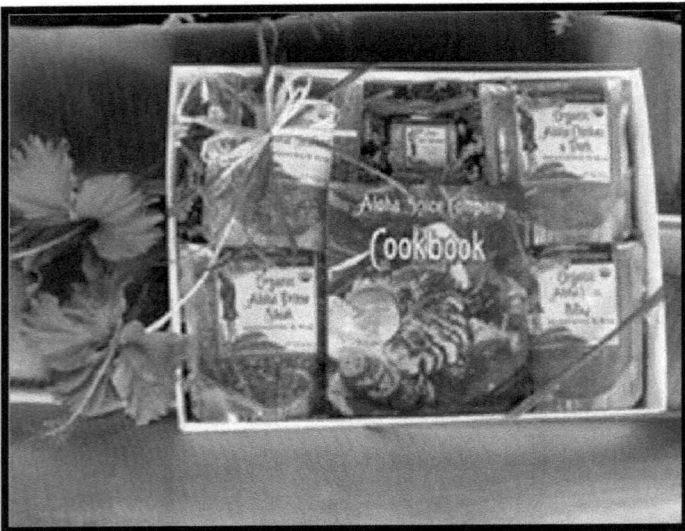
Gift sets are a popular offering from the Aloha Spice Company

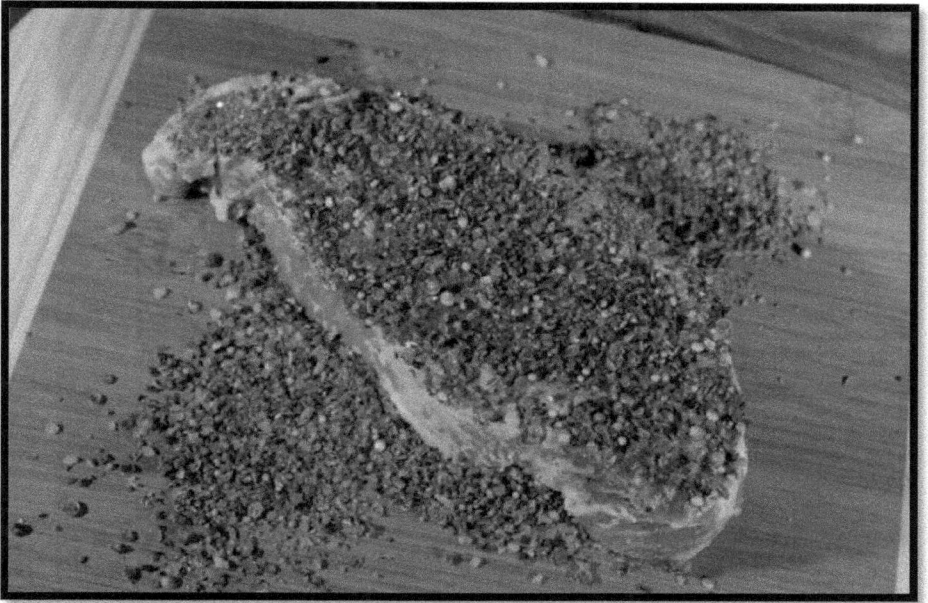
Product detail for Joanna's steak rub

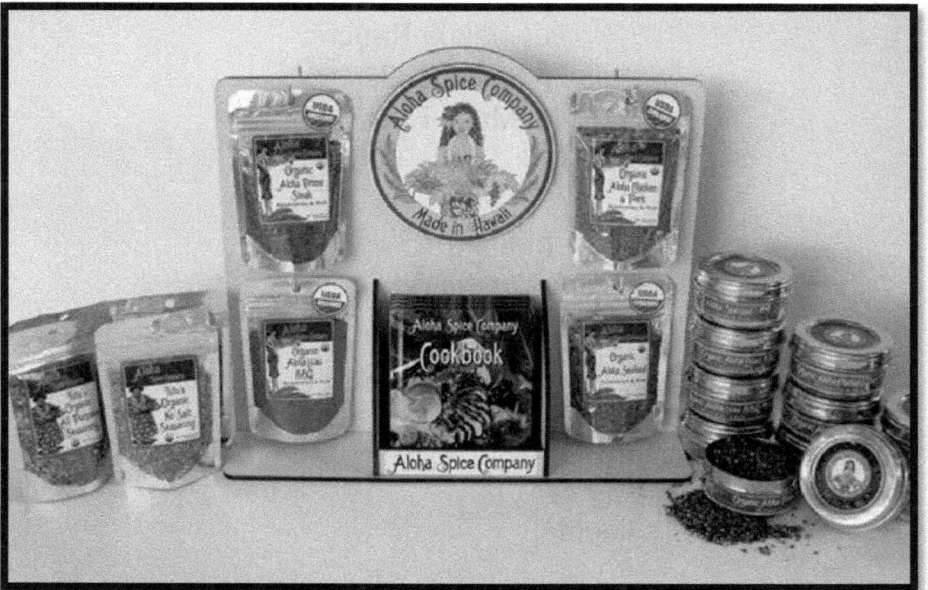
Aloha Spice Company product lineup

Chapter 25: Wine
Maui's Winery

Ulupalakua

VINEYARDS

Maui's Winery

Ulupalakua Ranch
Hawai'i 37
Kula, Maui, HI 96790
(808) 878 - 6058

mauiwine.com
info@mauiwine.com

Established
1974

Leadership
Paula Hegele, President

Products
Pineapple and grape-based wines

Don't shun the pineapple/embrace it...

For most people, the idea of living in Hawai'i is a dream. Inevitably, a vacation sparks romantic notions and ideas of "what if we could live here." It ends up being something many think about, but few actually get the opportunity to do.

Paula Hegele's story was different. She had the opportunity to move to Hawai'i, she just wasn't sure it was the right move for her, especially if she was going to be starting a family.

Paula was raised in the Puget Sound area of Washington. She met her future husband in college. After getting married, Paula's husband, who was raised in Hawai'i, wanted to go back home and began talking to Paula about a move to Maui.

Paula wasn't as sure. She liked Hawai'i during vacations/trips to visit relatives with her husband. She was taking a practical approach to life, though. Securing jobs was difficult, the cost of living was high, and what impact would this have on their children, if/when they had kid(s)? Would they get the same sort of well-rounded experiences she got living in Washington if they were raised on an island?

Paula's husband must be a great salesman because eventually he got her to cave in and make the move. He secured work in the hospitality industry, and they moved to Maui in 1980.

In hospitality, you often move around, especially early on in your career. The Hegeles moved to Kaua'i in 1982 and stayed until 1989 when another job transfer moved them back to Maui.

Even in their first stint in Maui, Paula found a favorite activity which finally helped her turn the corner about living in Hawai'i. She and her husband would leave their home and take a two-hour drive to the Upcountry region of Maui. This scenic drive offered a totally different topography than she had experienced there before. The combination of getting out and driving somewhere, and trees and fauna which was reminiscent of home in Washington, finally made Hawai'i feel like home for Paula.

One of her favorite stops in the Upcountry was Maui's Winery. Over the years, these frequent trips resulted in the Hegeles getting to know the staff. She soon developed a friendship with the general manager, and he asked her if she would like a job. Initially she declined, but he would continue to ask her over the years. Eventually, the timing was right, and the appeal of the job was strong enough that Paula accepted a position at the winery.

She was hired on as a part-time assistant to the general manager. It was an interesting time in the history of the company. Having opened in 1974, they were well ahead of the winery explosion which would sweep the country a few decades later.

The winery was struggling to find its identity and approach. It had been opened with the idea of developing a new industry for Hawai'i: a wine as respected as the vineyards of California. To get there, they would have to refine their processes for cultivating and growing in a climate in which it was difficult to grow grapes.

As the task of establishing a grape vineyard became more difficult even than originally anticipated, the team turned to a Hawaiian classic: the pineapple. This was despite the fact the owners believed a pineapple wine was more of a novelty than a respected product.

Pineapple was readily available and easy to work with. Heck, leave it on your counter too long, and it will start fermenting right there. The thought process was once they got their grape vineyard going, the pineapple line would be discarded.

An interesting thing happened on the way to becoming the "Southern California of the South Pacific"... even though the locals weren't attracted to yet another pineapple product, visitors, seeking true local products, liked Maui Winery's pineapple offerings. The taste was popular, and it was a product they were actually seeking when visiting a Hawaiian winery.

On the other hand, their line of grape-based wines struggled. Their Carnelian grapes, typically a high yielding, flavorful fruit, did not thrive in their soil/climate, and they were dealing with a disease strand which was difficult to diagnose.

Still, management had plans to set a sunset date on the pineapple wines (both a sparkling and a still), though nothing was off the table at this point. There was even the possibility they could close the vineyard, and focus solely on pineapple wine since it had proved to be so successful.

Hiring an experienced and successful person from the California wine industry would have probably been the ideal way to turn around Maui's Winery if the owners were committed to the long-term viability of the company. They were apprehensive since they believed they would likely be instructed to start again from scratch since what they were doing wasn't coming together.

With Paula entering into the situation and bringing an outsider's perspective, she was given a lot of latitude to bring ideas to the table to improve the brand. Initially, she was not given much in terms of financial support, so she sought to make small, inexpensive changes which could potentially make small improvements to the brands.

Her first step in making a small but noticeable improvement was to redesign the labels. Her idea was to have local artists design their labels. Industry insiders felt this was yet another step backwards for Maui's Winery since all of their bottles then had a completely different look (a uniform approach was the standard of the time). Of course, Paula was probably just a decade ahead of her time when you compare wine labels today with their bold looks and colors. Her decision to update the labels was a positive first step in getting the brand turned around.

Her next step was to simply convince management to embrace the pineapple. Yes, it doesn't have the same industry caché as a fine wine produced with grapes, but it truly was their cash cow. It kept the lights on. Her idea was warmly embrace the pineapple line and use the success and profits from those offerings to continue to improve their traditional wines.

After working with the University of Hawai'i and the University of California Davis, she made the tough decision to remove all of their Carnelian grapes and replant. She also decided to go with some lesser-known varietals of grapes for their other offerings. Her idea was to avoid chardonnay or merlot grapes since their product would always taste slightly different. If customers were comparing their chardonnays or merlots to what they had been drinking from other wineries, the wines would likely have a different flavor profile since the grapes would have been produced in the unique soil and climate of Hawai'i. She wanted to walk the delicate balance of securing product lines where the consumer was familiar with them, but not *too* familiar.

Paula faced the most difficult decisions yet when the Maui Land and Pineapple Company® announced it was shutting down. Strong competition from the Philippines and Taiwan meant there no longer would be a large-scale commercial pineapple industry in the State of Hawai'i. Paula would be challenged with either importing pineapple or discontinuing the product line she had worked so hard to keep.

Working with state and local representatives, other local businesses, the owner of the local Ulupalaukua Ranch and a group of experienced pineapple growers, managers and executives, the group was successful in keeping 1,000 acres of pineapples so Maui-based businesses could utilize locally sourced pineapple. This ensured that the famous Maui Gold™ pineapple was available for the local fruit market.

In the end, it translated to a higher quality product for Maui's Winery. Rather than having the pineapples juiced offsite as they had previously, they now did all of the juicing themselves. The result was an improved and highly flavorful juice as the base for their pineapple wine products.

Visitors to Maui's Winery enjoy a much improved tasting room over the one Paula had experienced when she started visiting. They get to experience a historic facility featuring a cottage where King Kalākaua himself had hosted parties back in the 1870s. The cypress trees which formed the hula circle have been carved into statues on the grounds. They also feature artwork from the artists who have designed the labels. Guests can taste their wines and stroll the grounds on their own, or they can go on guided tours. They also have a restaurant, the Ulupalakua Ranch Grill®, right across the street offering local favorites.

The winery benefits from the fact they have no seasonality. The weather is always great in Maui, and they welcome visitors the entire year. Over the years their grape wines have vastly improved, and they have finally started to receive industry recognition and awards for their offerings.

Reflecting back, Paula is pleased to have made the move to join the Maui's Winery organization and to have made the move to Hawai'i in the first place. She's found a place that is warm, exciting and fun to live and work. She has raised three boys in Hawai'i, and her initial concerns have proven to be totally unfounded. Rather than completely isolated being raised on an island, she feels her children have benefitted from a cultural awareness they wouldn't have received had they stayed in Washington.

Whether it's a gift or a decoration in a home, the pineapple is largely regarded as a symbol of hospitality. With all it has meant to her personally and professionally, few can attest to that fact more than Paula Hegele.

Maui's Winery Photo Album

Paula Hegele

The scenic drive to Maui's Winery is one of the first things to draw Paula to the company

The Tasting Room at Maui's Winery

Where the magic happens: the vineyard

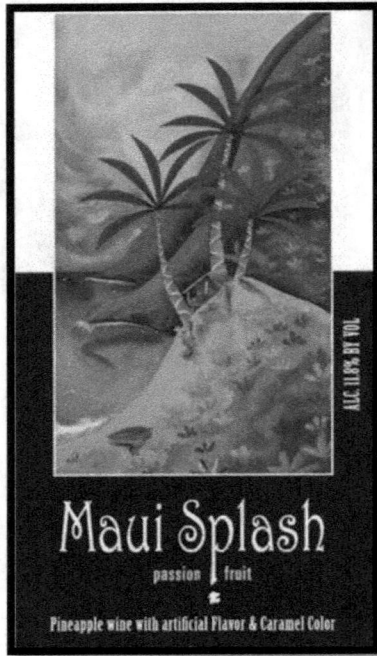

Maui Splash
passion fruit
Pineapple wine with artificial Flavor & Caramel Color

ALC. 11.8% BY VOL.

One of Paula's first ideas was to bring the work of local artists to the labels of Maui's Winery products

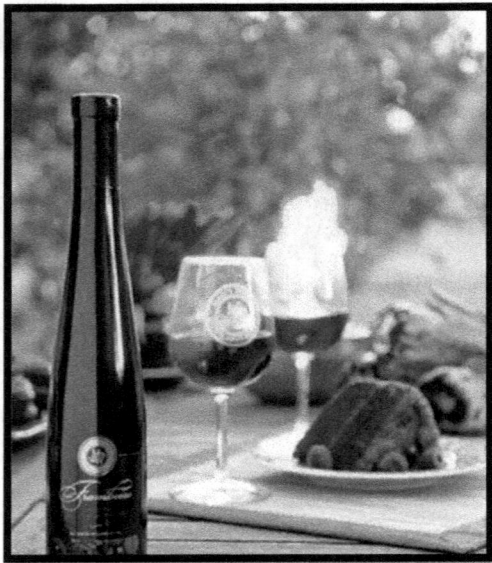

Here's a party you want to be invited to!

Soon to be wine!

Maui's Winery product lineup

Author's Notes/Resources

The stories of the small companies featured in the **Small Brand America** series are always incredibly fascinating to put together. To me, the stories of the people behind these brands are equally as fascinating as the stories of the actual products.

Adding the element that all brands here are made in Hawai'i is an extra twist which makes them even more interesting. Most are available throughout Hawai'i if you are visiting. Many can be bought over the internet as well. Continued success may mean they may soon be in a grocery store near you.

I do suggest learning more about the companies featured in the book and their products. The more you know about them, and the hard work they are doing to try to get to know you, the more you are likely to try their products. You might just find something you like better than the same brands you've always purchased, simply because "you've always purchased them."

Here's an "Island Guide" showing the websites for each:

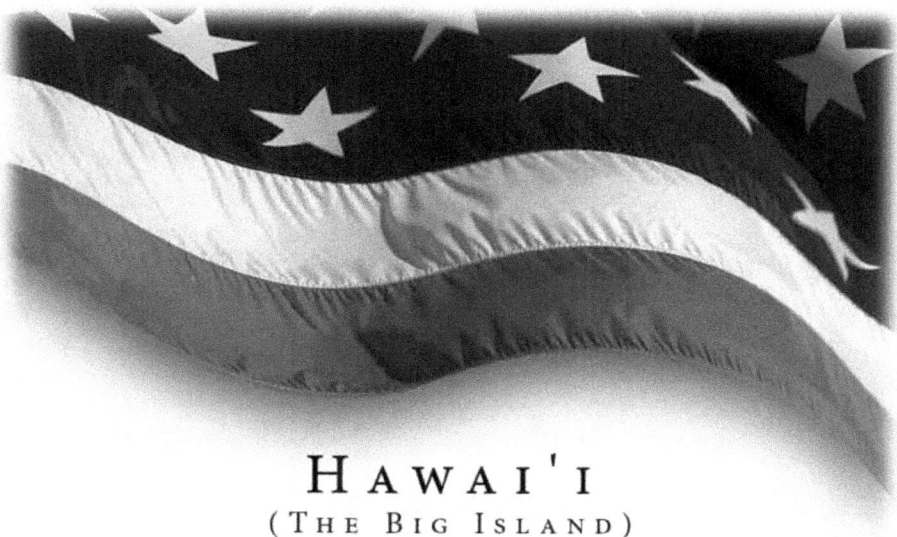

HAWAI'I
(THE BIG ISLAND)

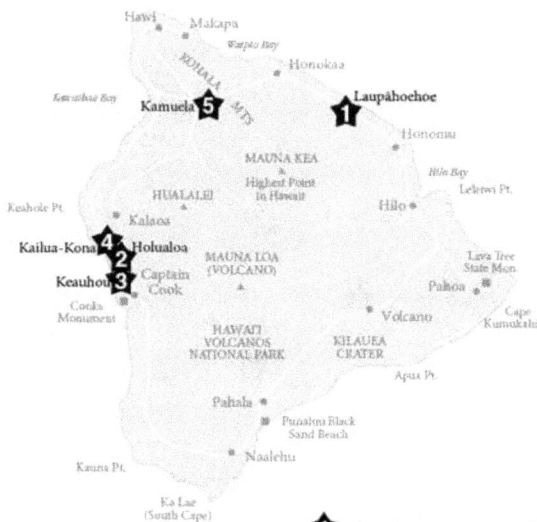

1. **Hamakua Mushrooms** ★ Laupāhoehoe
   hamakuamushrooms.com
2. **Hula Daddy Kona Coffee** ★ Holualoa
   huladaddy.com
3. **Kona Natural Soap** ★ Keauhou
   konanaturalsoap.com
4. **Original Hawaiian Chocolate** ★ Kailua-Kona
   ohcf.us
5. **Tropical Dreams Ice Cream** ★ Kamuela
   tropicaldreamsicecream.com

KAUA'I

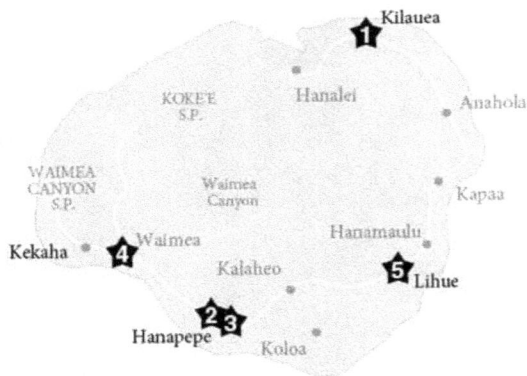

1 **Akamai Juice Company** ★ Kilauea
   akamaijuice.com

2 **Aloha Spice Company** ★ Hanapepe
   alohaspice.com

3 **Anahola Granola** ★ Hanapepe
   anaholagranola.com

4 **Aunty Lilokoi Products** ★ Waimea
   auntylilikoi.com

5 **Kōloa Rum** ★ Lihue
   koloarum.com

MAUI

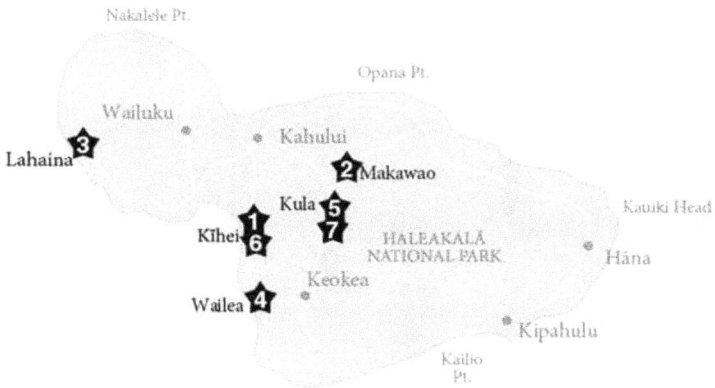

1. Adoboloco ★ Kihei
   adoboloco.com
2. Haliimaile Distilling Company ★ Makawao
   haliimailedistilling.com
3. Maui Brewing Co. ★ Lahaina
   mauibrewingco.com
4. Maui Dog Treats ★ Wailea
   dogtreatsmaui.com
5. Maui's Winery ★ Kula
   mauiwine.com
6. Shaka Pops ★ Kihei
   shakapopsmaui.com
7. Surfing Goat Dairy ★ Kula
   surfinggoatdairy.com

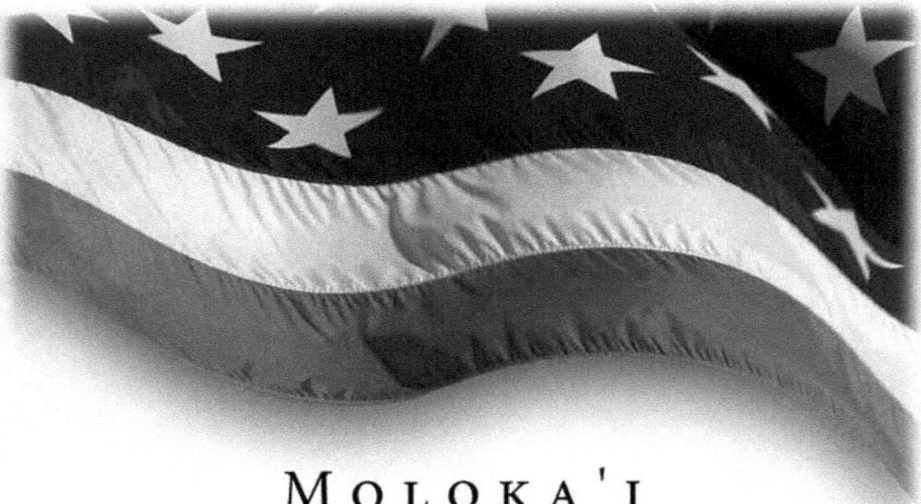

MOLOKA'I

1 Moloka'i Mele ★ Kaunakakai
realhawaiiahoney.com

O'AHU

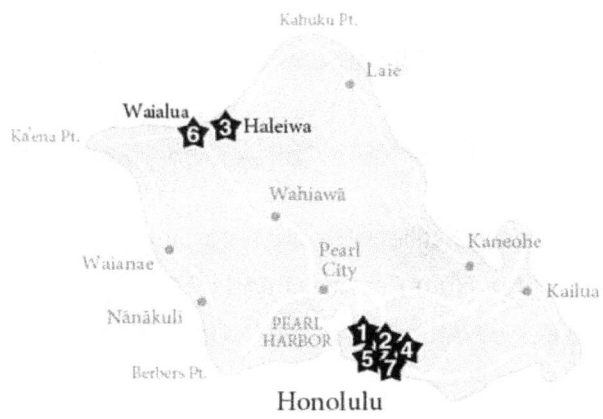

1. **Da Secret Sauce** ★ Honolulu
dasecretsauce.com
2. **Govinda's Fresh Juice** ★ Honolulu
govindasjuice.com
3. **Hawaii's Special, Inc.** ★ Haleiwa
hawaiisspecial.com
4. **Island Distillers** ★ Honolulu
islanddistillers.com
5. **Minato Hawai`i** ★ Honolulu
minatohawaiiangift.com
6. **North Shore Goodies** ★ Waialua
northshoregoodies.net
7. **Sea Salts of Hawai`i** ★ Honolulu
seasaltsofhawaii.com

Bibliography/Sources

In addition to the websites of the companies profiled (all listed in the **Author's Notes/Resources** section), the following resources were also utilized to create this book:

Interview with Adoboloco Owner Tim Parsons: 1/30/14.

Interview with Akamai Juice Company Owner Cas Schwabe: 12/30/13.

Interview with Anahola Granola Owner Becky Burns: 1/27/14.

Interview with Aunty Liliko'i Products Owner Lori Cardenas: 12/30/13.

Interview with Da Secret Sauce Owner Rex Moribe: 1/19/14.

Interview with Govinda's Fresh Juices CEO Jim Eicher: 12/22/13.

Interview with Haliimaile Distilling Company Master Distiller Mark Nigbur: 11/19/13.

Interview with Hamakua Mushrooms President Bob Stanga: 1/8/14.

Interview with Hawaii's Special President Dave Delventhal: 2/2/14.

Interview with Hula Daddy Kona Coffee Owner Karen Paterson: 12/30/13.

Interview with Island Distillers Proprietor Dave Flintstone: 12/16/13.

Interview with Kōloa Rum President and CEO Bob Gunter: 1/3/13.

Interview with Kona Natural Soap CEO Greg Colden: 1/20/14.

Interview with Maui Brewing Co. Founder Garrett W. Marrero: 12/27/13.

Interview with Maui Dog Treats Owner Heidi Cramer: 2/6/14.

Interview with Maui's Winery Owner Paula Hegele: 12/13/13.

Interview with Minato Hawai'i Owner Mac Takeda: 1/28/14.

Interview with Moloka'i Mele Managing Partner Brenda Kaneshiro: 1/2/14.

Interview with North Shore Goodies Owner Marc Bryner: 1/4/14.

Interview with Original Hawaiian Chocolate Founder Pam Cooper: 11/21/13.

Interview with Shaka Pops Owners Christine Vestfals and Larry Lutz: 1/31/14.

Interview with Sea Salts of Hawaii Proprietor Sandra Gibson: 11/11/13.

Interview with Surfing Goat Dairy Owner Thomas Kafsack, 1/13/14 & 1/14/14.

Interview with Tropical Dreams Ice Cream President John Edney: 1/7/13.

Lyrics to the song: *Insane in the Brain* © Cypress Hill.

Photographs
All photographs, in the sections of each business featured, have been utilized with permission from the respective companies with the following exceptions:

Original Hawaiian Chocolate®
All Original Hawaiian Chocolate photos are copyrights of Produce to Product, Inc.

Da Secret Sauce
Cody Stewart (Rex working), Josiah Paterson (Da Secret Sauce bottle, First Batch, Production & Kaya Paterson) & Ryan Beppu (Rex Bodyboarding & BBQ)

Hawaii's Special, Inc.
The shot Dave at Pupukea Gardens is courtesy of Edwart Rameriz Photography

Shaka Pops
The shot of the boy eating the pop (Ashton Guvenir) entitled, "You can get Shaka Pops at an event..." courtesy of Down Guvenir and the shot of Larry and Christine with the bike is courtesy of Teresa Reiss

Special Thanks

- ☺ To my mom, Sandy Akley, for her help in editing this book.
- ☺ Thanks to my wife Amy and to my daughter Cat for just being themselves.
- ☺ To Melanie Roller, my friend and special Hawaiian consultant for Steve Akley publishing.
- ☺ Hats off to Mark Hansen (*mappersmark@gmail.com*) for the great cover design and maps of the Hawaiian Islands. He's the greatest graphic artist you will ever find!

The following individuals from the featured companies not only couldn't have been nicer, without their help this book would not have been possible:

- ☺ Marc Bryner, North Shore Goodies
- ☺ Becky Burns, Anahola Granola
- ☺ Tony & Lori Cardenas, Aunty Liliko'i Products, LLC
- ☺ Pam and Bob Cooper, Original Hawaiian Chocolate
- ☺ Greg Colden, Kona Natural Soap
- ☺ Marty Corrigan, Kona Natural Soap
- ☺ Heidi Cramer, Maui Dog Treats
- ☺ David Delventhal, Hawaii's Special, Inc.
- ☺ John Edney, Tropical Dreams Ice Cream
- ☺ Jim Eichler, Govinda's Fresh Juices
- ☺ Dave Flintstone, Island Distillers
- ☺ Sandra Gibson, Sea Salts of Hawaii
- ☺ Bob Gunter, Kōloa Rum Company
- ☺ Paula Hegele, Maui's Winery
- ☺ Thomas Kafsack, Surfing Goat Dairy
- ☺ Brenda Kaneshiro, Moloka'i Meli, LLC
- ☺ Larry Lutz, Shaka Pops
- ☺ Garrett W. Marrero, Maui Brewing Co.
- ☺ Mark Miller, Produce to Products, Inc.
- ☺ Rex Moribe, Da Secret Sauce
- ☺ Mark Nigbur, Haliimaile Distilling Company
- ☺ Tim Parsons, Adoboloco
- ☺ Tyler Reams, North Shore Goodies

- ☺ Angela Reichert, Surfing Goat Dairy
- ☺ Cas Schwabe, Akamai Juice Company
- ☺ Robert Stanga, Hamakua Mushrooms
- ☺ Mac Takeda, Minato Hawaii
- ☺ Jeanne Toulon, Kōloa Rum Company
- ☺ Christine Vestfals, Shaka Pops
- ☺ Lani Weigert, Hamakua Mushrooms

Lastly, lots of love for my father, Larry Akley. He's always with us in spirit.

Dad's badge

In Loving Memory of Larry Akley
1942 – 2012

Dad at Old Faithful

Dad's badge photo compliments of Kelly Brooks (thanks sis!)

About the Author

Steve Akley is a lifelong St. Louis resident. He lives with his wife Amy, their daughter Cat and a 22 lb. Maine Coon cat named Leo.

The family enjoys travel, Christmas music, watching NFL football and spending weekends at their second home: a log cabin in a lake community about an hour south of their home. Steve reports that the entire family shares his fondness for small brands trying to make it in the United States, Hawai'i... and ice cream.

Steve's other interests include: bourbon, Starbucks®, the art of SHAG, the Red Hot Chili Peppers, blueberries, huckleberries, growing chili peppers, the music of Dick Dale (*dickdale.com*), chicken wings, turtles/tortoises, hawks, banana slugs, Abraham Lincoln (same birthday as Steve), Harry Truman (Missouri's only president), everything St. Louis, New Mexico, Florida, Maine (best blueberries), poker/card games, Seinfeld, Quentin Tarantino movies, metal advertising signs and bacon.

Small Brand America III is his eighth published work, but he has lots of other great book ideas. Sign up for his newsletter, or check out his latest work, on his website: *steveakley.com*. Steve also maintains an author's page on *Amazon.com*. Just search his name on the site.

Steve can be reached via email: *info@steveakley.com*

Find Steve on Social Media

@steveakley

Follow Steve to see what he's up to!

WORDPRESS

http://steveakley.wordpress.com

Steve posts weekly updates about his writing projects on his blog. You can sign up to have his weekly posts emailed to you!

Steve Akley

Like Steve's page on Facebook

Love A Cat Charity – Honolulu, Hawai'i

Steve Akley proudly supports the mission of Love A Cat Charity with a donation from the proceeds of the sale of all of his books.

Mission Statement

Love A Cat Charity's mission is to help end euthanasia of unwanted cats by caring for feral and abandoned felines, spaying or neutering them and, when appropriate, adopting them out. Love A Cat Charity emphasizes the use of Trap-Neuter-Return (TNR) technique to humanely control feral cat populations. Cats are humanely trapped, spayed or neutered and returned to their outdoor homes. TNR improves the cats' health and stabilizes the colony while allowing them to live out their lives outdoors. No new kittens are born and the cats no longer experience the stresses of mating and pregnancy.

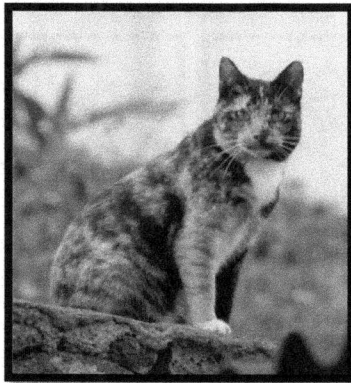

Support of Love A Cat Charity in Honolulu, HI, helps cats like this sweet kitty

Love A Cat Charity
P.O. Box 11753
Honolulu, HI 96828
loveacatcharity.org

Also by Steve Akley

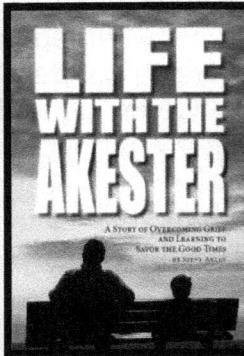

Steve's Website

Steve's website is the hub for information about his work, where to find his books and a means to reach out to him. Through his website, he has a sign-up to receive his newsletter which he publishes four times a year (March 1, June 1, September 1 and December 1). To learn more about his books, and to sign-up for his newsletter, check out:

www.steveakley.com